- - FEB 1993

This book is to be returned on or before
the last date stamped below.

821·4

12 NOV 1993

THE LANGUAGE OF LITERATURE
General Editor: N. F. Blake

Published titles

An Introduction to the Language of Literature   N. F. Blake
The Language of Shakespeare   N. F. Blake
The Language of Chaucer   David Burnley
The Language of Wordsworth and Coleridge   Frances Austin
The Language of Irish Literature   Loreto Todd
The Language of D. H. Lawrence   Allan Ingram
The Language of Thomas Hardy   Raymond Chapman
The Language of Drama   David Birch
The Language of Jane Austen   Myra Stokes
The Language of the Metaphysical Poets   Frances Austin

Further titles are in preparation.

Other books by Frances Austin

The Letters of William Home Clift 1803–1832   (Meldon House)
Robert Clift of Bodmin: Able Seaman 1790–1799   (Meldon House)
The Clift Family Correspondence 1792–1846   (The Centre for English Cultural Tradition and Language, University of Sheffield)

The Language of the
Metaphysical Poets

FRANCES AUSTIN

MACMILLAN

© Frances Austin 1992

All rights reserved. No reproduction, copy or transmission of this publication may be made without written permission.

No paragraph of this publication may be reproduced, copied or transmitted save with written permission or in accordance with the provisions of the Copyright, Designs and Patents Act 1988, or under the terms of any licence permitting limited copying issued by the Copyright Licensing Agency,
90 Tottenham Court Road, London W1P 9HE.

Any person who does any unauthorised act in relation to this publication may be liable to criminal prosecution and civil claims for damages.

First published 1992 by
THE MACMILLAN PRESS LTD
Houndmills, Basingstoke, Hampshire RG21 2XS
and London
Companies and representatives
throughout the world

ISBN 0-333-49566-7 hardcover
ISBN 0-333-49567-5 paperback

A catalogue record for this book is available from the British Library.

Typeset by LBJ Enterprises Limited
of Chilcompton and Tadley

Printed in Hong Kong

Contents

Prefatory Note	vii
Acknowledgements	ix
Grammatical Terminology	xi
Note on Texts	xiii
Chronological Chart	xiv
1 Introduction	1
2 John Donne (1572–1631)	18
3 George Herbert (1593–1633)	47
4 Richard Crashaw (1612–49)	75
5 Henry Vaughan (1621–95)	100
6 Thomas Traherne (1637–74)	127
7 Analysis of Passages	155
8 Conclusion	166
Appendix 1 Hermetic Philosophy	172
Appendix 2 The Cambridge Platonists	176
Notes	178
Select Bibliography and Further Reading	185
Index 1 Literary and Historical References	189
Index 2 Language Topics	191

For
JEAN
who gave me my first book of poems
and
PATRICIA
who taught me 'grammar'

Prefatory Note

Such phrases as 'metaphysical poetry' and 'metaphysical poets' ('the metaphysicals') are widely used and understood but it is hard to define them. Dryden first used the term 'metaphysical' in this context in 1693 in *A Discourse Concerning the Original and Progress of Satire*. Praising the poems of the Earl of Dorset, he said that Donne 'affects the metaphysics ... and perplexes the minds of the fair sex with nice speculations of philosophy'. What this means is not clear, but the word stuck. Pope is said to have called Donne's poetry 'metaphysical' (*Spence's Anecdotes*, 1744). His opinion of it may best be understood from a section of his *Imitations of Horace* (1737): 'The Satires of Dr John Donne, Dean of St Paul's, Versified'. Better known is Johnson's grouping, in his 'Life of Cowley', of a number of the seventeenth-century poets as 'metaphysical poets' (*Lives of the Poets*, 1779-81).

Etymologically, 'metaphysical' means 'behind or beyond the physical'. It is also defined as 'being concerned with first principles and the essence of Being and Knowing'. Such notions neatly encompass the work of the religious and meditative poets Donne, Herbert, Crashaw and Vaughan, whose verse is the subject of this short book.

In whatever light we set these poets, however, Donne and his poetry stand out. Until the twentieth century the word 'metaphysical', when used in discussions of English poetry, was abusive and it is clear that it was Donne's poetry that called this forth. Likewise, twentieth-century comment on the metaphysical poets gives Donne's work far more space and consideration than that of the other three poets here named. A reason for this may be suggested. Herbert, Crashaw and Vaughan – the same goes for Traherne, the fifth of our poets – are religious and meditative writers whose secular verse, where it exists, is of far less importance. Donne's religious poetry, however, even when what may be called his philosophical poetry is added to it, does not amount to half of his poetical output. Furthermore, his secular poetry is still widely read – perhaps even more widely read than his religious verse. Much of this secular poetry was written in the 1590s and the first decade of the seventeenth century, before most of the religious verse, and it is in this early work that Donne first used the linguistic features that are the hallmark not only of his own poetry but of that of much of the later metaphysical poets also. To discuss the language of Donne's poetry without reference to his secular verse would be unreasonable and I have therefore widened my brief to take it in. Many of Donne's religious poems are sonnets and it would not be possible to demonstrate fully from this form alone those features of dramatic and conversational tone that depend on metrical variation.

Traherne's poetry has been read only since its first publication in 1903. Yet he died long before Vaughan and his subject matter is wholly religious. It therefore seemed worth while to examine his poetry within the context of the generally acknowledged – if vague – metaphysical canon. The language of religious devotion gives common ground for comparison. Because Traherne's poetry was composed after the Commonwealth and he is in some ways isolated from the more closely-knit earlier group, I have adopted a slightly different way of looking at his language from that used for the other four poets.

East Stour, Dorset　　　　　　　　　　　　　　　FRANCES AUSTIN
October 1990

Acknowledgements

In the course of writing this book I have been fortunate to have the help and encouragement of friends and colleagues. Helen Wilcox has supplied me with much bibliographical information; Katie Wales has phototcopied articles and sent books that I could not obtain elsewhere; Bernard Jones has read and re-read the various drafts and made many suggestions; and John Gibson has painstakingly read through the whole script. To all these people I am most grateful. They are not, of course, responsible for any errors or shortcomings. As always, Professor Norman Blake has been a firm and faithful support.

I am also much indebted to the staff of Sherborne County Library and the Dorset Inter-Library Loan Service for their time and patience in tracing and borrowing books. Without their assistance this book could not have been written.

Grammatical Terminology

Inevitably in a book of this kind grammatical terms must be used even if they are kept to a minimum. Some readers may be unfamiliar with even 'traditional' terminology and others may be used to different terms of the various current grammatical 'models'.

In this book, the traditional terms for the 'parts of speech' – noun, verb, adjective, etc. – have been used. For describing the basic sentence or clause structure the model of Systemic Grammar has generally been followed. Subject, Verb and Complement (S V C) are the main syntactical groups that make up the clause. The term Complement includes both the Object and Complement of 'traditional' grammar. Subjects and Complements are often 'realised' by nominal groups. A nominal group is a group of words centred on a noun which is called the 'head' of the group. An example is 'the cross little girl with black curls which look like corkscrews'. *Girl* is the 'head' of the group; the words coming before are pre-modifiers and those after make up the post-modification. Premodifiers are usually single words. Post modifiers are often prepositional groups, such as *with black curls*, or clauses, usually relative clauses: *which look like corkscrews*. Complements are also 'realised' by adjectives or adjectival phrases when they follow the verb *to be* or other copular verbs such as *seem*. Verbs are 'realised' by verbal groups. These may consist of a single verb or a verb preceded by one or more auxiliary verbs. 'Her mother *smacked* her' is an example of the first kind and 'I *would have smacked* her if I had been her mother' of the second. Note that the verb which conveys the 'main' information (called a 'lexical' or 'lexically full' verb) comes last in the group. The other main groups in a clause are adverbials, either single words such as *happily* or adverbial

xi

groups such as *with her doll*; *for a while*. Adverbials can occur in strings, as in 'She played *happily / with her doll / for a while'*.

It is now customary in Systemic Grammar to discard the term 'sentence' and substitute 'clause complex'. Readers will find both terms used in this book. 'Sentence' seems too useful a term to be rejected completely, but at times 'clause complex' is clearer and more precise because it indicates the clause structure of which the sentence is composed and the way in which those clauses are put together.

Most books based on Systemic Grammar mark the verbal group with a P for Predicator. V seems more accessible to those unfamiliar with this model, so it has been adopted here. An exposition of Systemic Grammar will be found in Dennis Freeborn, *A Course Book in English Grammar* (Macmillan, 1987). A useful introductory book on grammar that shows the relation of traditional grammar to the Systemic model is N. F. Blake, *Traditional English Grammar and Beyond* (Macmillan, 1988).

For grammatical terms and explanations other than those used in Systemic Grammar, I have used Randolph Quirk *et al.*, *A Comprehensive Grammar of the English Language* (Longman, 1986). Definitions of rhetorical terms and further information on them may be found in Katie Wales, *A Dictionary of Stylistics* (Longman, 1989). A book in this series that covers most aspects of the language and terminology used is N. F. Blake, *An Introduction to the Language of Literature* (Macmillan, 1990).

Note on Texts

The poems of each of the five poets examined here have been quoted from the Oxford English Texts editions. Details of individual volumes will be found in the Bibliography. For Traherne, the edition by Gladys Wade (1932) has also been used and readers are recommended to consult it for the sequence of Traherne's poems as the arrangement is clearer than that in Margoliouth's edition (1958). In the chapter on Vaughan I have drawn extensively on the notes in the edition of Alan Rudrum (1976). Further comments on manuscripts and text status are included in the first note for each chapter where appropriate.

Quotations from Sidney and Spenser in Chapter 1 are taken from the Oxford English Texts editions: *The Poems of Sir Philip Sidney,* ed. William A. Ringler Jr (Oxford: Clarendon Press, 1962); *Spenser's Faerie Queene,* ed. J. C. Smith (Oxford: Clarendon Press, 1909, repr. 1978) 2 vols. The edition used for quotations from Shakespeare is *William Shakespeare: the Complete Works,* eds Stanley Wells and Gary Taylor (Oxford: Clarendon Press, 1986).

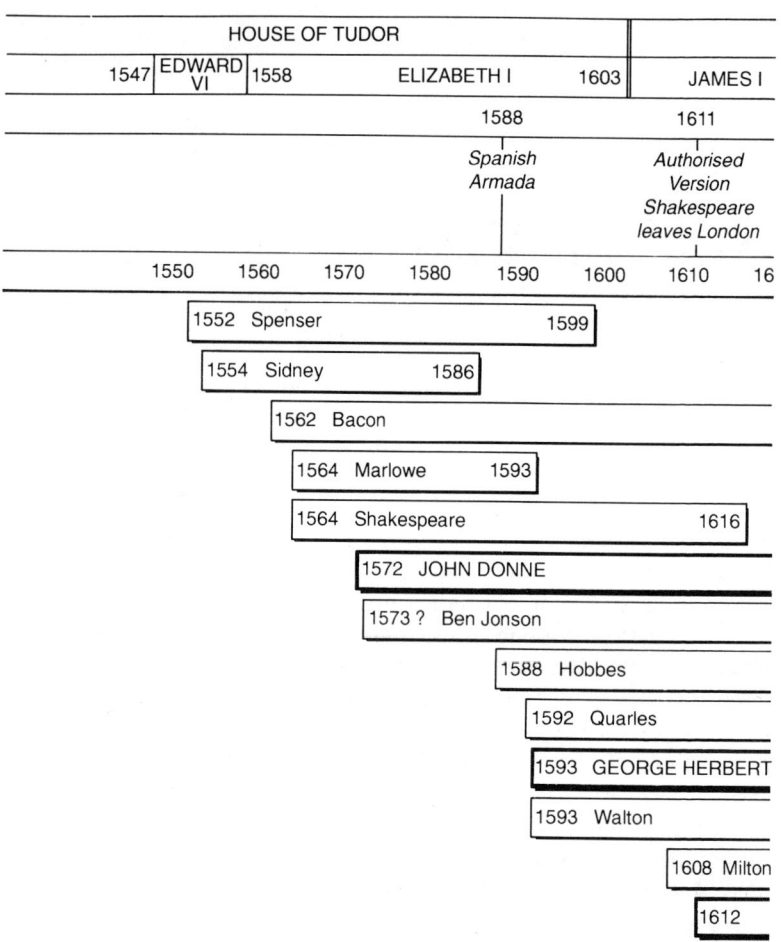

Chronological Chart

INTRODUCTION xv

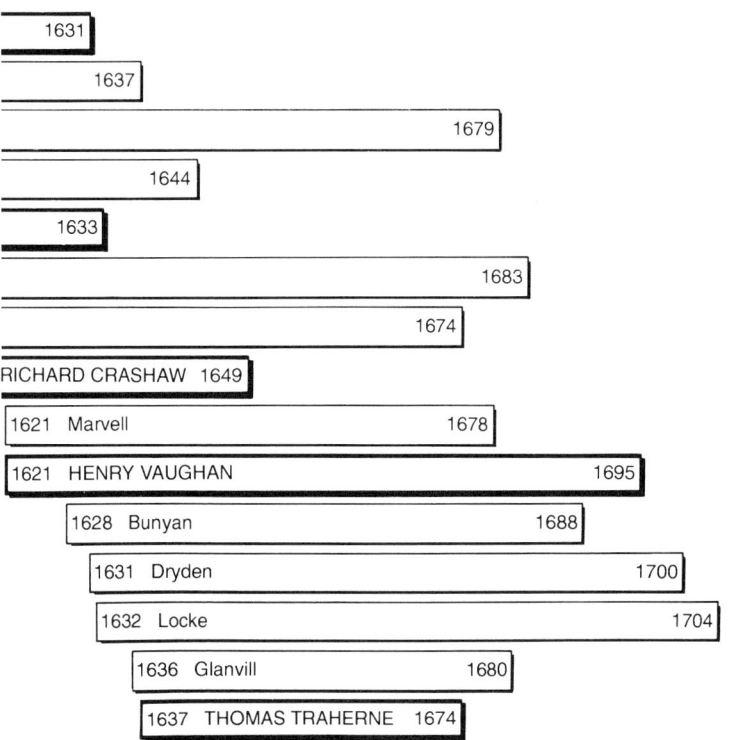

1 Introduction

The lives of the five poets examined here span over a hundred years. John Donne was born in 1573, fifteen years before the Armada (1588), and Henry Vaughan died in 1695, seven years after the Glorious Revolution (1688) that marked the end of effective Roman Catholic claims to the British crown. They encompass the turbulent years of the four Stuart kings, the Civil War and the Commonwealth. The politico-religious uncertainty of this period was further disturbed by new ideas in science and philosophy. The seal was set on these by the discoveries of Galileo in 1609, but in the previous century Copernicus had unleashed the notion of a planetary system that circled the sun. The first significant indication of the new learning in England was the publication of Bacon's *Advancement of Learning* (1605). The inductive method of reasoning that Bacon outlined in this work was enlarged in later parts of the unfinished *Instauratio Magna*, notably *Novum Organum* (1620), and led to the founding in 1660 of the Royal Society.

Uncertainty in all spheres of life conditioned the religious verse written in the first half of the seventeenth century. The change in values and attitudes made for an intellectual climate in which men examined their consciences more closely and took stock of their own position in relation to Church and State. Such heart-searchings (recorded by Izaak Walton) as those of Donne, whose Roman Catholic background hindered his secular career, led to religious poetry of an intensely personal kind.

Hobbes's *Leviathan* (1651) was above all a call for the end of civil unrest and bloodshed and a return to some sort of political authority. Such authority, however, was by this time far removed from that which had ruled the medieval world. The divine right of kings, which had been carefully fostered by the Tudors, but so unhappily asserted by the ill-fated Charles I, was no longer acceptable even in the thesis of Hobbes, tutor to the future Charles II. Hobbes's materialistic work was written and published in the middle of the century, during the Commonwealth. Although it expressed an ethic that had been growing since the time of Elizabeth it pleased no party. Hobbes was called 'atheist', although he might more correctly have been described as a 'deist'. Unlike his predecessor Descartes (1596–1650) he rejected the notion of the 'soul' as a separate entity, existing apart from the body. He did not reject the truth of the Bible or religion but they were included only by some falling back on casuistry. Such supra-material matters were necessarily relegated to the periphery by his empirical idea of truth.

Philosophers, no longer bound by the dogma of medieval schoolmen, lined up with the new scientists who advocated empiricism. Church doctrine, which dealt only with things that could not be weighed and measured, was no longer paramount. A wedge had been driven between things spiritual and material. Although it was not foreseen at the time, the seeds were already sown for the division of power between Church and State. After the Restoration in 1660 the time for personal reflection was over. Henceforth, religious writers would adopt a more public stance in both prose and poetry.

This shift from the private and devotional nature of religious verse can be found in the work of Milton, who wrote both before and after the Commonwealth. His *Poems* of 1645 contain several pieces from his very early years. None is in the very personal style of the metaphysical poets but two are on biblical subjects later selected by Crashaw. 'On the Morning of Christ's Nativity' and 'On the Circumcision' must have been known to the younger poet, although not surprisingly he treats them in a very different way. So the Puritan Milton and Catholic Crashaw meet. Apart from a couple of paraphrases from the Psalms, Milton's other poems of this date have little in common with metaphysical poetry and come nearer perhaps to Spenser earlier and the later 'Cavalier' poets. *Comus*, too, which was performed in 1634, shows Milton the courtier. After the outbreak of the Civil War, and indeed before, Milton published prose tracts on matters of public concern. His vast poetic works appeared only after the Restoration. In these the Puritan moralist and public mentor replaced the earlier poet who had revelled in the sheer lyric music of words. The description of Hell in *Paradise Lost* (1667) can be seen as a veiled picture of the Restoration Court. The man of affairs that Milton became during the Commonwealth was not abandoned when he turned once more to poetry. Similarly, the world portrayed in Bunyan's *Pilgrim's Progress* (1678) is intended as a condemnation of society in the last quarter of the century. Dryden, too, at the end of the century, adopted the role of critic of public life in both poetry and plays. Even his personal dilemma of Church allegiance was conducted as a public debate in *The Hind and the Panther* (1687). Matters of conscience were by this time expressed in a general manner that foreshadows the eighteenth-century poetry of the Enlightenment.

Of the many writers of religious verse in the first half of the seventeenth century few are read today. The rest, some of considerable merit, time has condemned to oblivion. Of those whose names are still known, Donne, Herbert, Crashaw, Vaughan and Traherne have been selected for examination here. Donne, Vaughan and Crashaw wrote secular verse and love lyrics as well as religious poetry, but only the secular poems of Donne have been included in this volume.

These five poets are linked in several ways. Apart from Crashaw, they are all of Welsh descent. Vaughan's mother-tongue was Welsh and, coupled with reading of Welsh poetry, it almost certainly affected his English usage. Some idiosyncracies that appear in his verse have been noted by his biographers but other features of his verse are also attributable to his being Welsh-speaking.[1]

Apart from Vaughan, all took holy orders. Crashaw was an Anglican, whose leaning towards Rome unsteadied him at Cambridge. The consequences of the death of Charles I took him into the Roman Church. Donne, on the other hand, was a Roman Catholic by upbringing, who after much reading and thought became an Anglican and, as Dean of St Paul's, rose to be the most eminent public figure of the five. As a young man, Herbert sought secular preferment before he turned to the Church. Traherne, too, may have hoped for some high Church office after he left his Herefordshire living to become private chaplain to Sir Orlando Bridgeman, Lord Keeper of the Seal to Charles II. But some five years later the king stripped Bridgeman of his position and Traherne shared in the collapse of the family fortunes.

The Civil War directly affected the careers of only Crashaw and Vaughan. The vagaries of Court, however, affected the other three. At the beginning of the century, Donne's expectations of secular office were cut short by his marriage to Ann More, the niece of Sir Thomas Egerton, whose secretary he was and who, like Sir Orlando Bridgeman, was Keeper of the Seal. For marrying Ann More, Donne was dismissed. After a brief time in prison and years of poverty, he embraced Anglicanism and found favour with James I. James persuaded him to take orders in 1615 and in 1621 made him Dean of St Paul's.

Herbert's ambitions, on the other hand, were wrecked by the death of James in 1625 and, like Donne, but for different reasons, he also reluctantly entered the Church. Unlike Donne he neither sought nor gained high office and retreated upon the small parish of Bemerton near Wilton, the Herberts' family seat, where he spent his last three years ministering to his country parishioners. Herbert left a record of his secular disappointments, notably in 'Affliction' (I):

> Whereas my birth and spirit rather took
> The way that takes the town;
> Thou didst betray me to a lingring book
> And wrap me in a gown.
> (11.37–40)

The War drove both Crashaw and Vaughan into exile. Crashaw had been elected Fellow of Peterhouse College, Cambridge, in about 1636. In 1644, however, he found he could not conscientiously comply with the Puritan régime and fled to Holland and thence to Paris. There he made the final break by entering the Roman Church. Eventually, he was recommended to the Pope by Henrietta Maria, the exiled queen, and received a minor post at Loreto in Italy. Like Herbert, he did not live long after entering on this new phase of his career and he died in unclear circumstances in 1649. Crashaw was the most obvious scholar of the five poets and was temperamentally suited to the life of a College Fellow.

Vaughan, too, was a fugitive from the War. The son of a Royalist family, in 1642 he was called home to Wales from

London, where he was reading law. Thus his career was wrecked at its outset. Whether or not he himself served in the Royalist army is uncertain, but his friends, including his former teacher and his twin brother, were ejected from their livings and his beloved younger brother, William, died prematurely, possibly from injuries sustained in the fighting. Thereafter, Vaughan lived the rest of his life – over forty years – as a recluse in his native countryside, where he practised medicine. That he cut himself off altogether from worldly affairs, however, is contradicted by records of family law-suits. Of the metaphysical poets, he alone lived into the new era of stability after the accession of William of Orange and Mary, the Protestant elder daughter of James II.

Much of the religious poetry of these five poets was written during their late twenties and thirties. For Herbert, Crashaw and Traherne these were the last years of their lives. Herbert and, perhaps, Crashaw finally found peace of mind in holy orders. Herbert conveys the greatest sense of writing within the framework of an established Church. Crashaw's most memorable poems are those in which he contemplates with apparent ecstasy some aspect of Christ's life or that of a saint. Traherne seems never to have undergone such agonizings of spirit as Herbert and Crashaw. His last years were marked by an unexpected preferment, followed by a complete reversal and obscurity. Changes of fortune, however, do not show themselves in his poems. The inner joy, or 'felicity' as he called it, that he pursued throughout life shines through all his writings alike in prose and verse. Both Donne and Vaughan lived to a greater age than the others and much of their religious verse was, therefore, written in middle life. Donne wrote the majority of his religious lyrics, as well as the longer pieces, before he entered the Church. Perhaps for this reason the lyrics especially reveal an intense and questioning mind. Vaughan, the only one who did not ultimately find a place in the Church, worked out a personal salvation through poetry. Of the vast number of his poems on widely differing aspects of religion, those that are concerned with his personal experience speak to the reader most convincingly. Vaughan's experience was clearly different from Donne's. The poems are less dramatic and have that mystical quality that makes them seem more detached from self in spite of their very personal nature.

The language of the seventeenth-century metaphysical poets differs from that of preceding poets and the break starts with

Donne. But his language and that of his successors necessarily grew out of styles in vogue in his youth. Donne was an Elizabethan by birth and upbringing and wrote his earliest poems, including at least some of *Songs and Sonets*, before the turn of the century. It would be unthinkable that he owed nothing to the Elizabethan tradition. Even when he is turning against it, his poetry, both in treatment of subject matter and language, has affinities with that of the Elizabethan poets. Likewise, many of the apparently 'new' attitudes and linguistic features of his poetry can be found earlier. Some of these features need to be examined to see how they developed from the poems of major Elizabethan poets such as Sidney, Spenser and Shakespeare.

Donne was not alone among the poets (and also playwrights) of the 1590s and first decade of the new century to turn to a plainer style. Indeed, the plain as opposed to the eloquent style was not new in English poetry but stemmed from medieval didactic and moral verse. It was first applied to the lyric by Wyatt, who used it to express anti-courtly attitudes to the Petrarchan love convention.[2] It was not much adopted in the strictly Elizabethan period except for satirical verse. Early and mid-Elizabethan poets preferred the rhetorical and courtly style – often over-courtly – that was possible once the English language was felt to be sufficiently eloquent.[3] Some of the Elizabethans, notably Shakespeare but also Sidney and Ralegh, affected to repudiate courtly attitudes and style but while criticizing it they continued to write within its conventions. Various reasons have been suggested for a change at the end of the century. One is the move away from a court-based poetry. Unlike Sidney, Ralegh and Spenser, the new and younger poets were not courtiers. They were by birth or education, like Donne, aspirants to public office. They tended to gather round the Inns of Court, which became in effect a training ground for a 'civil service'. In these circumstances it was not surprising that there was a move away from the language of courtly ritual. Indeed, Donne's language has been described as 'Inns of Courtly rather than courtly'.[4]

Every so-called revolution in poetic language calls itself a return to language based on speech and everyday usage. The shift in style of the 1590s was no exception. Herbert, whose earliest years were also influenced by the Elizabethan tradition, left some comments on poetic language in two poems entitled 'Jordan'. In these he states his belief in the plain style. 'Jordan' (II) begins:

When first my lines of heav'nly joyes made mention,
Such was their lustre, they did so excell,
That I sought out quaint words, and trim invention.
(11.1–3)

The 'quaint words' and 'trim invention' were part of the Elizabethan notion of eloquence that Herbert, like Donne, sought to avoid. A factor in the plain style adopted by Donne is his everyday vocabulary and the wide range of reference to objects and topics of current interest, which replace the classical allusions of predecessors such as Sidney. Naturally, everyday words can be found in Sidney and the other Elizabethan poets. A large part of any verse is necessarily made up of them. It is the deliberate avoidance of the 'eloquent' or 'sugared' diction that distinguishes Donne's style. *Songs and Sonets*, in particular, relies heavily on native monosyllabic vocabulary – in his longer poems Donne uses more Latinate words and vocabulary of Romance origin – and overall his diction sounds prosaic and 'flat' beside that of Sidney, Spenser and Shakespeare.

Closely related to such vocabulary are colloquialisms. These, too, can be found in the love lyrics of earlier Elizabethan poets but less often than in Donne's *Songs and Sonets*. The colloquial element in the earlier poets is rarely found in isolated words and is, moreover, obscured by obsolescent words and older grammatical forms, such as the pronouns *ye* and *thou*, and the *-th* ending of the third person present singular. These were already becoming archaic and their non-appearance in Donne makes his language seem much more modern. Sidney usually indicates colloquial language by context. In Sonnet 15 of *Astrophil and Stella*, in which the lover repudiates the Parnassian, various phrases, such as 'the ribs of old *Parnassus*' and 'poore *Petrarch*' are intended to be colloquial. The deliberate mocking of alliteration in 'running in ratling rowes' in the same sonnet also indicates colloquialism, as does the line, which includes a proverbial-type saying – always an indication of low usage: 'And sure at length stolne goods do come to light'. In the game of 'Barley-brake' in 'A shepheard's tale' from the 1593 *Arcadia*[5] there are a number of colloquial, or conversational-sounding lines, such as 'To crammed mawes a spratt new Stomake brings' (1.134) and, when Pas strikes Cosma, she 'Up with hir fist, and tooke him on the face' (1.274). There is, too, a fair sprinkling of colloquial words: *snugging*; *micher*; *brawlings*; *back-parts* and *chapps*. This poem, which is intentionally written with 'no height of stile', is, in spite of the fact that it also includes many phrases belonging to the pastoral convention, something of an exception, mixing both high and low styles. Usually, Sidney's diction is much more decorous than Donne's. Shakespeare, too, in his non-dramatic verse is usually elegant and stately, although again colloquialisms appear occasionally in the sonnets.

Another of Herbert's comments on language, which comes in 'Jordan' (I), seems to refer to the Elizabethan pastoral tradition:

> Is it no verse, except enchanted groves
> And sudden arbours shadow course-spunne lines?
> Must purling streams refresh a lovers loves?
> (11.6–8)

As Herbert's lines indicate, he rarely uses the language of Elizabethan pastoral and neither is it found in the poems of other metaphysical poets. Donne, especially, and Herbert, too, set their poems in the world of affairs in which they lived. The 'painted' world of pastoral and Elizabethan love poetry is generally missing and with it goes the description found in the pastoral. Donne's language is not descriptive or visual in this sense. We find none of the 'chery lipps', 'milke hands' or 'golden haire' ('A shepheard's tale') of the ladies (or shepherdesses); the piping shepherds, who complain in 'sigh-broken ditties' (*'Philisides'*) or 'leape with joy and jolitie' ('A shepheard's tale'), according to their mood; the 'merry flockes' (*Astrophil and Stella*, 'Ninth song') of 'silly sheepe' (*Countess of Pembroke's Arcadia*, Third Eclogues, 63, 'Let mother earth'); the landscape in which they are placed: the groves 'most rich of shade' (*Astrophil and Stella*, Eighth song), 'flowry fieldes' (*'Philisides'*) and birds with their 'wanton musicke' (*Astrophil and Stella*, Eighth song, 'In a grove'). All the stage machinery of the pastoral that Herbert implies in his lines in 'Jordan' (I) has gone. These examples are all taken from Sidney but others can be found in Spenser and Shakespeare. Shakespeare, with his usual instinctive insight and grasp of all kinds of language, mocked this style in *A Midsummer Night's Dream* (c.1596) in the play performed by the 'rude mechanicals':

> *Thisbe:* These lily lips,
> This cherry nose
> These yellow cowslip cheeks
> Are gone, are gone.
> Lovers, make moan.
> (V.I.325–9)

In some of his sonnets, too, Shakespeare makes negative use of courtly language. One instance is Sonnet 130:

> My mistress' eyes are nothing like the sun;
> Coral is far more red than her lips' red.
> If snow be white, why then her breasts are dun;
> If hairs be wires, black wires grow on her head.
> I have seen roses damasked, red and white,
> But no such roses see I in her cheeks.[6]
> (11.1–6)

This counter courtly expression, with its perverse use of colour, still, however, relies on the vocabulary of the pastoral and courtly love poem. Nearer to Donne's abstract but plain style is the language Shakespeare uses in Sonnet 138:

> When my love swears that she is made of truth
> I do believe her though I know she lies.
> (11.1–2)

Sidney intellectualizes courtly and eloquent language (for argument) in *Astrophil and Stella* but he does not, as Shakespeare does here and elsewhere, adopt the abstract and rather 'flat' diction typical of Donne's style of argument.

The final two lines of the stanza already quoted from Herbert's 'Jordan' (I), are:

> Must all be vail'd, while he that reades, divines,
>   Catching the sense at two removes?
> (11.9–10)

In the following and final stanza of this poem Herbert continues this theme: 'Riddle who list for me'. However, much early metaphysical poetry, including Herbert's, contains an element of riddling, which conceals as well as expresses the meaning. Donne's arguments often involve paradox based on 'chop logic' and syllogistic reasoning. Both of these have their source in the epigram tradition. The classical syllabus for Elizabethan schoolboys included translation of epigrams from Latin – Martial was a favourite – and the composition of epigrams, both Latin and English.[7] Donne, and later Crashaw, both wrote epigrams in English and it is evident that the compressed, riddling style found its way into their other poetry. An example of Donne's use of this type of writing is:

> If any who deciphers best,
>   What we know not, our selves, can know,
> Let him teach mee that nothing; This
> As yet my ease, and comfort is,
> Though I speed not, I cannot misse.
>   ('Negative Love' 11.14–18)

These lines, especially the last, have the cryptic reasoning of epigram. This, too, can be found in the Elizabethans, although it appears less and is not so tersely expressed. Sidney writes in Sonnet 61 of *Astrophil and Stella*:

> Now since her chast mind hates this love in me,
>   With chastned mind, I straight must shew that she
> Shall quickly me from what she hates remove.
>   O Doctor *Cupid*, thou for me reply,
>   Driv'n else to graunt by Angel's sophistrie,
> That I love not, without I leave to love.
>   (11.9–14)

The following Sonnet (62) is similar. Stella bids Astrophil guide his love by 'Virtue', to which he replies:

> Alas, if this the only mettall be
>   Of *Love*, new-coind to helpe my beggery,
> Deare, love me not, that you may love me more.
>   (11.12–14)

In these examples the final lines of each sonnet are, like Donne's, epigrammatic in the paradoxical and inverted nature of the argument. However, the reasoning in the example from Donne is closer-knit. It does not rely on such overt metaphor as the second example from Sidney, nor does it include the classical apostrophe of the first.

Donne's analytic expression necessarily affects both vocabulary and syntax but the extent to which he uses them for argument has often been exaggerated. He does argue through words and syntax but no more than through juxtaposition of statements and analogies. He uses a great many conjunctions of the *if ... then*, *as ... so* type but these are frequent in earlier Elizabethan love poetry. The *as ... so* frame indicates simile and usually occurs in conjunction with the conceits for which Donne is noted. Sometimes, as in the celebrated 'compasses' conceit, he uses a concrete image but the conceit itself works on an abstract or logical level. This marks a difference between Donne's conceits and those of the earlier Elizabethans. Complex conceits are found in Sidney but at their most subtle they remain firmly in a concrete if idealized world, as in Sonnet 44 of *Astrophil and Stella*:

> I much do guesse, yet find no truth save this,
> That when the breath of my complaints doth tuch
> Those daintie dores unto the Court of blisse,
> The heav'nly nature of that place is such,
>   That once come there, the sobs of mine annoyes
>   Are metamorphosd straight to tunes of joyes.
>   (11.9–14)

Although somewhat obscured by circumlocutory metaphorical expression, the conceit is essentially physical. Sidney's conceits are concrete and 'pretty' in a way that Donne's are not. For Sidney this conceit is unusually lengthy. Donne, however, frequently sustains a conceit or variations on it through a whole poem, as in 'The Flea'. Other examples are 'A Jeat Ring Sent', 'A Nocturnal upon S. Lucies Day' and 'Aire and Angels'.

In the sixteenth century, epigram and conceit come together in emblems. Emblem books were essentially books of pictures that had explanatory, often moral, verses attached to them.[8] They were popular in Tudor England, although no book of emblems was published here until 1586. This was Geoffrey Whitney's *A Choice of Emblemes*, an anthology drawn from the various books already printed abroad. The pictures were usually conventional and abstract rather than representational. Part of their appeal lay in the 'wit' by which apparently unconnected ideas were linked. The reader was presented with a puzzle, rather, as Rosemary Freeman says, like the clues to a crossword puzzle or the way in which illustrations to advertisements are intended to tease the reader's curiosity by their apparent irrelevance.[9] The words 'wit' and 'conceit' occur frequently in contemporary criticism of the emblem books. The epigram tradition, deriving in this instance from Greek, occurs in the 'mottoes' that were incorporated in or round the picture, and in the accompanying verses. Donne frequently uses emblems obliquely and allusively, whereas Herbert uses them overtly. The influence of the tradition, however, is found everywhere in both secular and religious writing and not only in verse. Some of Donne's conceits are taken directly from emblems. The most obvious, again, is the 'compasses' image. Compasses represented constancy.

This was a well-known emblem and was the imprint of Christopher Plantin, the French printer who produced many editions of emblem books in Antwerp. Antwerp was the home of the best engravers at the time. Plantin's editions became widely known in England and Donne could not have been unaware of them. Donne's most celebrated conceit, therefore, was not original.

Spenser is the Elizabethan poet whose work demonstrates most extensively the popularity of the emblem. Emblems appear in all his work from the earliest verse to *The Faerie Queen*, where it is most obvious in the personifications of moral qualities. *Occasion* is described with two of her conventional attributes: a long forelock, by which she might be seized, and an otherwise bald head:

> Her lockes, that loathly were and hoarie gray,
> Grew all afore, and loosely hong vnrold,
> But all behind was bald, and worne away.
> (Book II, canto iv, stanza 4)

Another clearly emblematic description is that of *Ambition*:

There, as in glistring glory she did sit,
   She held a great gold chaine ylincked well,
   Whose vpper end to highest heauen was knit,
   And lower part did reach to lowest Hell;
   And all that preace [press] did round about her swell,
   To catchen hold of that long chaine.
                    (Book II, canto vii, stanza 46)

Sidney's use of emblems is less obvious. Traces of them appear in the poems in *Arcadia*. In 'A shepheard's tale' the mark that Klaius chalks on the shoulders of himself and Strephon is clearly emblematic:

(His marke a Piller was devoid of stay,
   As bragging that free of all passions' mone
   Well might he others beare, but leane to none).
                                         (11.70–2)

In 'My sheepe are thoughts' from Book II of *Arcadia* Sidney introduces an instance of the explanatory verse that was part of the emblem. The picture that would have accompanied these lines is not hard to visualize:

My sheepe are thoughts, which I both guide and serve:
Their pasture is faire hilles of fruitlesse Love:
On barren sweetes they feede, and feeding sterve:
I waile their lotte, but will not other prove.
My sheepehooke is wanne hope, which all upholdes:
My weedes, Desire, cut out in endlesse foldes.
                                         (11.1–6)

The last two lines have the epigrammatic quality that frequently clinches an argument in such verses, although they lack the terseness of a true epigram:

What wooll my sheepe shall beare, whyle thus they live,
In you it is, you must the judgement give.
                                         (11.7–8)

A few emblems occur in the prose, notably in the various

'devices' on the helmets of the knights. Heraldic devices were associated with the emblem convention and heraldry, of course, is emblematic in its very conception. Emblems are rare in *Astrophil and Stella* but one sonnet that relies heavily on heraldic devices is Sonnet 13:

> *Jove's* golden shield did Eagle sables beare,
> Whose talents held young *Ganimed* above:
> But in Vert field *Mars* bare a golden speare,
> Which through a bleeding heart his point did shove.
> (11.3–6)

Shakespeare uses emblems occasionally. Ophelia's comments on each of the flowers she distributes in the mad scene in *Hamlet* are in the emblem tradition. Flowers, like heraldic devices, had their particular meanings. Another instance, in which Shakespeare mocks the tradition, occurs again in the play of the 'rude mechanicals' in *A Midsummer Night's Dream*. When Moonshine enters, carrying his lantern, thorn-bush and dog, the significance of the last two is never known because, after his initial statement that 'This lantern doth the hornèd moon present', the courtiers interrupt until Moonshine forgets his lines and reverts in exasperation to prose:

> All that I have to say is to tell you that the lantern
> is the moon, I the man i' th' moon, this thorn bush my
> thorn bush, and this dog my dog.
> (V.i.252–4)

Such examples are typical of the use that Elizabethan writers made of emblems in literature. They appear in every sphere of art, particularly the visual arts, from architecture to embroidery. By the time Donne was writing, the tradition was moving from a public and conventional mode to a more personal, often religious, and inner form of expression, best exemplified in England by the emblem books of Francis Quarles.[10] The usage progressed through various stages of change until, by the time of the Commonwealth, the cast of mind which caused the popularity of the emblem book had virtually disappeared. Influenced by Baconian empiricism, people looked more to the experience of their senses for understanding life, both physical and spiritual. It is not surprising, therefore, that emblems, the embodiment of accepted and conventional truths deriving from the medieval world, are used more loosely in the poetry of Vaughan and do not figure at all in the writings of Traherne.

Instruction in rhetoric constituted the chief part of Elizabethan education. After the publication in 1553 of Thomas Wilson's *Art of Rhetorique*, manuals for guidance in composition were printed in English as well as Latin, and this accounts for an upsurge in rhetorical and over-rhetorical writing. Shakespeare parodied this in *Love's Labour's Lost* (c. 1594). Again, in 'Jordan' (II), Herbert attacks the rhetorical mode of writing that he himself first used. Following his remarks on 'quaint words' quoted earlier he continues:

> My thoughts began to burnish, sprout, and swell,
> Curling with metaphors a plain intention,
> Decking the sense, as if it were to sell.
> (11.4–6)

Apart from metaphor, which Herbert continued to use and which, indeed, is part and parcel of the metaphysical conceit, all the metaphysical poets employed many of the rhetorical figures beloved of the Elizabethans, and none more so than those that incorporated word play. The various means of repetition, in particular, are used by all of them and are inherent in the epigrammatic style of Donne. Not surprisingly, the figures of repetition are found extensively in the Elizabethan poets. Repetition of vocabulary and structure can be found in the examples from Sidney's sonnets quoted above (p.10). The first of these also includes a pun. Sidney's word-play, however, is almost always light-hearted and not often associated with serious argument and syllogism, as it often is in Donne. Frequently it is no more than simple statement, as in Sonnet 60 of *Astrophil and Stella*:

> Then some good body tell me how I do,
> Whose presence, absence, absence presence is:
> Blist in my curse, and cursed in my blisse.
> (11.12–14)

The chiastic repetition of words and syntax (*antimetabole*) is typical of Sidney and is usually simply ornament.

A feature of Donne's poetry that is often remarked on is its dramatic quality. This derives from its basis in speech. It has usually been ascribed to the ruggedness of his metrical usage and the shifts of stress that he sometimes employs. These, however, have been over-emphasized. The dramatic openings *in medias res* of many of the lyrics in *Songs and Sonets* are often over-emphasized. This dramatic quality has been thought original to Donne and a departure from the tradition of earlier Elizabethan poetry, although it can be found earlier still in the poetry of Wyatt. However, we have only to turn to Sidney's *Astrophil and Stella* to find dramatic expression. Sidney often changes mood from sonnet to sonnet. This type of dramatic effect is achieved by his ability to create the sense of a speaking voice through written language. An example of change of mood occurs from Sonnet 63 to Sonnet 64, although there is a song in between. The first sonnet shows a light-heartedness in playing with the possibilities of grammatical rules for the purpose of forwarding the courtship of Stella:

> For Grammer sayes (ô this deare *Stella* weighe,)
> For Grammer sayes (to Grammer who sayes nay)
> That in one speech two Negatives affirme.
> (11.12–14)

The mood is indicated not only by the frivolous subject matter but through the syntax. The repetition of *For Grammer sayes* followed by breaks before the expected clause complements, together with the direct and provocative address to Stella, convey the teasing humour of the poem. It is a convincing representation of speech in the literary mode and the reader both hears and *sees* the lover's attitude. There is a sharp change of mood in the opening lines of the sonnet that follows the song:

> No more, my deare, no more these counsels trie.
> O give my passions leave to run their race.
> (11.1–2)

The excited anticipation engendered by the interruption of the statement in the previous sonnet gives way to a mood of resigned patience. This is achieved, at least partly, by the same device of repetition, although the parenthetical address to his mistress does not this time interrupt the flow of the main statement and is not provocative in intention. Sonnet 47 is another dramatic miniature. Here too, the scene is expressed through dramatic-type verse but is of a different kind from the preceding examples:

> Let her go. Soft, but here she comes. Go to,
> Unkind, I love you not: O me, that eye
> Doth make my heart give to my tongue the lie.
> (11.12–14)

Clearly, the actual speech of the scene is imaginary but the interior monologue of the vignette is convincing and near in kind to that in some of Donne's pieces. Donne is more energetic and consistently dramatic than Sidney but Sidney shows that he was as much a 'frequenter of plays' as the younger poet and had learned from them how to introduce their method into verse not written for the stage. One difference between Donne's use of the dramatic and that of the Elizabethan love poets is that whereas the Elizabethans usually sustain a part through a sequence of poems (this is particularly true of the sonnet sequences) Donne shifts both his *persona* and his attitudes to women from poem to poem. Equally important is the distancing effect imparted to the drama by introducing pastoral features within the courtly convention. Donne, however, brings the dramatic encounter close to both speaker and reader.

A few of the chief linguistic features of Donne's poetry and some that are also associated with the later metaphysical poets have been selected here to show that the seeds of their main characteristics were sown by earlier poets. Nevertheless, Donne's verse is so distinctive, even in some of these areas, that his poetic voice could hardly be mistaken for that of Sidney or any other Elizabethan poet. This may be attributed partly to his personal use of stress and rhythm, which have only been mentioned in passing in this chapter. Donne's use of language is, indeed, as individual as that of each of the later metaphysical poets. This can now be examined in detail.

2 John Donne (1572–1631)

> *'as infinite, as none'*
> Holy Sonnet 'Oh, to vex me'

Two aspects of Donne's language have often been commented on and both are part of his rhetoric: his unusual handling of metre and his images. These last are thought to characterize any poetry that is termed 'metaphysical'. Donne's subject matter is inseparable from the language in which it is written and the different facets of the language themselves are intertwined in such ways that it is hard to isolate any one of them for examination. However, for the purposes of analysis and description it is necessary to try.

It is easy to assume that the core of Donne's vocabulary is dictated by the striking images of the similes and metaphors that run through his verse. Like all thinking men of the time Donne was aware of the new learning and there are, indeed, many words taken from subjects of contemporary interest. Examples of these, mostly from *Songs and Sonets*, are, from geography: *cosmographers*; *map*; *globes*; *straits*; *torrid zone*; *equinoctial*; *antipodes*; *southwest discovery* (i.e. the south-west passage), and many place names, such as *Nile*; *Egypt* and *Virginia* (then being colonized); from medicine and anatomy: *hydroptic*; *blood*; *bladder*; *heart*; *ventricle*; *muscle*; *brain* and *medicine* and *anatomy* themselves; from business: *coin*; *minted*; *angel* (in the sense of a coin); from botany: *engrafted*; *propagation*; *transplant*; *root*; from science or pseudo-science: *chemist*; *elixir*; *alchemy*; from war: *bullet*; *chain-*

shot; *pike*; *soldiers*; *bulwarks*; and from the law: *law* itself; *jointure*; *divorce*; *executor*; *legacies*.

Although Donne was interested in the 'new' Copernican cosmology, in his poetry he, like Milton, mainly falls back on the old Ptolemaic ideas of the universe. He does not name Copernicus or Galileo, although he does use the image of a telescope in the *Obsequies to the Lord Harington*:

> Though God be truly'our glass, through which we see
> All, since the beeing of all things is hee,
> Yet are the trunkes which doe to us derive
> Things, in proportion fit, by perspective,
> Deeds of good men; for by their living here,
> Vertues, indeed remote, seeme to be nere.
> (11.35–40)

The word *trunks* was at the time used of telescopes.[1] Philosophy is often the entire vehicle for the substance of an argument for part or the whole of a poem. It is not easy, however, to demonstrate this by citing individual words. 'Philosophy', at this time, generally meant knowledge of all kinds but in Donne's poetry it refers to ideas about the cosmos and this area, too, yields many words: *galaxy*; *spheres*; *constellations*; *meteors*; *planets*; *stars*; *concentric*. Words cited out of context do not always indicate the way they are used in poems. For example, the word *blood* does not necessarily imply an interest in physiology or medicine: it is often used in poetry in connection with blushing or the old belief that man was composed of the four elements that corresponded to the four humours. Donne uses the word with the meaning of 'to blush':

> her pure and eloquent blood
> Spoke in her cheekes, and so distinctly wrought,
> That one might almost say, her bodie thought.
> (*The Second Anniversarie*, 11.244–6)

However, when we read in the same poem:

> Knowst thou how blood, which to the hart doth flow,
> Doth from one ventricle to th'other go?
> (11.271–2)

the context, plus the collocation with *ventricle, hart* and *flow* implies a medical usage. The circulation of the blood was a subject of much debate at the time and would shortly be resolved by William Harvey.[2]

Donne's eclectic vocabulary takes in much besides topical subjects. As in most writings of the time words of many types and their derivatives find a place in his verse. Like the pamphleteers of the 1590s, Nashe, Greene and Gabriel Harvey, he does not eschew colloquialisms. Most words of this kind occur in the *Satyres* and *Elegies*, which were written about the time the pamphleteers were busy. The term 'elegies' here signifies the verse form – heroic couplets – in which the poems were written, not the subject matter. Examples of words of a colloquial, or even vulgar, type are the verbs *gull*; *belch*; *spew*; *spit*; *stink*; and the nouns *sweat*; *clog*; *whore*; *harlot*; *bawd*; *botch* and *pox*. Again, instances of single words give less idea of the colloquial nature of the writing than do whole lines:

> Or let me creepe to some dread Conjurer,
> Which with fantastique schemes fullfills much paper,
> Which hath divided Heaven in tenements,
> And with whores, theeves and murtherers stuft his rents.
> ('The Bracelet', 11.59–62)

Out of context words such as *creepe* and *stuft* do not sound particularly colloquial but they suit well with the unsavoury tenor of the matter dealt with in this poem. Satyre 2, 'Sir; though (I thanke God for it) I do hate', uses explicitly vulgar vocabulary:

> But hee is worst, who (beggarly) doth chaw
> Other wits fruits, and in his ravenous maw
> Rankly digested, doth those things out-spue,
> As his owne things;' and they are his owne, 'tis true,
> For if one eate my meate, though it be knowne
> The meate was mine, th'excrement is his owne.
> (11.25–30)

Less remarked on is the lyrical element in Donne's poetry. This ought not to surprise us as a number of his songs were early set to music.[3] Lyricism, especially Donne's type, is also hard to demonstrate by individual words. It manifests itself in images, cadence and rhythm, as well as in the Petrarchan allusions familiar at the time. It can best be understood from reading entire poems, such as 'Sweetest love, I do not goe/For wearinesse of thee'. This poem, unusually, keeps to the lyric strain throughout and is one of the poems entitled 'Song'. Although Donne occasionally uses the conventional vocabulary of Elizabethan love poetry and images, such as spring; flowers; birds and all the background of the natural world which is often connected with the lyric, it is rarely sustained for more than a few lines. One example is part of a simile in the Elegie, 'To his Mistris Going to Bed':

> Your gownes going off such beauteous state reveales
> As when from flowery meades th'hills shadow steales ...
> (11.13–14)

This is conventional but it extends little beyond these two lines. Part of 'Loves Growth' uses vocabulary and images that might find a place in any love lyric:

> ... not greater, but more eminent,
>   Love by the spring is growne;
>   As, in the firmament,
> Starres by the Sunne are not inlarg'd, but showne.
> Gentle love deeds, as blossomes on a bough,
> From loves awaken'd root do bud out now.
> (11.15–20)

Nature images here, like the vocabulary, seem more in the lyric tradition than is usual in Donne. 'The Primrose' is similar, and in this instance the flower image runs through the whole of the poem. In these examples not only are diction and imagery lyrical but the rhythm is comparatively smooth as well.

The intellectual content of Donne's poetry can be inferred from the words he uses. There are a fair number of Latinate and Romance words. Occasionally he even takes words and phrases from their original sources and adopts them directly into the run of his sentence. *Quelque choses* (1.15) in 'Loves Usury' and *non obstante* (1.11) in 'Loves Exchange' are examples. The latter is a legal term which would have been used in its appropriate English register. However, Donne uses both as nouns, marking them with indefinite articles.

Examples of Donne's Latinate vocabulary are: *dissolution*; *vexation*; *discretion*; *disproportion*; *corruption*; *vicissitude*; *idolatry*; *simplicity*; *ingenuity*; *correspondency* and *prerogative*. These show that most of the borrowed words, whether taken directly from Latin or by way of French, are abstract, mostly abstract nouns, and that many of them end in the typical suffix *-ion*. A few verbs also occur: *transubstantiates*; *interanimates* and *annihilate*, but they are fewer than the nouns. Latinate words occur in all the kinds of Donne's verse although less in *Songs and Sonets*. They tend to come in clusters but they rarely exceed on average more than one to a line, even in the more serious poems. They are noticeable because of their length. Moreover, they are often words not associated with poetry, although they usually fit easily into the run of the verse, as in the elegie, 'The Perfume':

> By thee the seely Amorous sucks his death
> By drawing in a leprous harlots breath;
> By thee, the greatest staine to mans estate
> Falls on us, to be call'd *effeminate*;
> Though you be much lov'd in the Princes hall,
> There, things that seeme, exceed *substantiall*.
> (11.59–64) [my italics]

But Latinate and Romance words do not constitute a very large proportion of Donne's overall vocabulary. The fact that they are often used in noun rather than verb form would tend, if there were too many of them, to detract from the energy of the language. Too much nominalization makes for opacity and lack of pace. Verbs are the main-spring of action and movement in both prose and poetry and Donne's poetry is above all energetic. Latinate and Romance words are also mostly abstractions, which make the meaning less concrete and forceful. Furthermore, Latinate words are nearly always polysyllabic and more syllables are therefore weakly stressed. This further reduces the vigour of the language.

A characteristic feature of Donne's vocabulary, and one which offers wide possiblities for variation of stress, is the number of monosyllables. One or two critics have noted this in passing[4] but little attention has been paid to it. Lines composed wholly of monosyllables occur frequently, especially in *Songs and Sonets*, and less often in the *Holy Sonnets*. All Donne's verse forms contain a large number of monosyllables. Examples from the first lines of two of the *Holy Sonnets* are:

> Spit in my face yee Jewes, and pierce my side;

and:

> Show me deare Christ, thy spouse, so bright and cleare.

One of many from *Songs and Sonets* is the beginning of 'Loves Infinitenesse':

> If yet I have not all thy love,
> Deare, I shall never have it all.
> (11.1–2)

Never is disyllabic but it is of a kind with the others.

Monosyllabic vocabulary is not of one type only, however. We tend to assume that monosyllabic words are mostly concrete, especially when they are nouns. Words such as *rock*; *sky*; *stone*; *tree*; *bird* and *field* come to mind. This is true in much nature and love poetry, and Donne's poetry contains a considerable number of such words. The *Satyres*, in particular, use concrete vocabulary, and not always of the vulgar and colloquial type cited earlier. In Satyre III, 'Kind pity chokes my spleen', we find:

> those blest flowers that dwell
> At the rough streames calme head, thrive and prove well,
> But having left their roots, and themselves given
> To the streames tyrranous rage, alas, are driven
> Through mills, and rockes, and woods,'and at last, almost
> Consum'd in going, in the sea are lost.
> (11.103–8)

Here the vocabulary is of a kind associated with poetry: nature and lyric-type words. In Satyre IV, 'Well; I may now receive and die', there are words of a more domestic, down-to-earth sort:

> He knowes, who'hath sold his land, and now doth beg
> A licence, old iron, bootes, and egge-
> shels to transport.
>
> (11.103–5)

There can, indeed, scarcely be any verse without some concrete words. Donne's are often markedly concrete, although he also uses many monosyllabic abstract words. These often denote emotions, such as *hate*; *grief*; *fear* and *love*.

Adjectives are less prominent than nouns or verbs in Donne's verse.[5] In the main they are abstract and unremarkable. Typical are *pure*; *true*; *strange*; *new* and *good*. Occasionally there are more striking and energetic examples, as in the first stanza of 'The Sunne Rising', which contains *busie*; *unruly*; *sawcy* and *sowre*. Donne also uses some learned adjectives. *Concentric*; *hydroptic*; *pedantic* and *extrinsic* are examples. He also occasionally has compound adjectives, the best-known of which come in the unusually lengthy nominal group from the Elegie, 'The Perfume': 'The grim eight-foot-high iron-bound serving man' (1.31). Another comes in a verse letter 'To the Countesse of Huntingdon' ('Man to Gods image'):

> As such a starre, the *Magi* led to view
>   The manger-cradled infant, God below.
>
> (11.13–14)

An unusual one that he uses more than once and is composed of native elements is *through-shine*, a word that would have delighted William Barnes and Gerard Manley Hopkins. In 'A Valediction: of my Name in the Window' its meaning is literal:

> 'Tis much that Glasse should bee
> As all confessing, and through-shine as I;
>
> (11.7–8)

but in one of the verse letters 'To the Countesse of Bedford' ('Honour is so sublime') it is metaphorical:

> This [your body], as an Amber drop enwraps a Bee,
> Covering discovers your quicke Soule; that we
> May in your through-shine front your hearts thoughts see.
>
> (11.25–7)

Although some, such as these, are striking, compound adjectives occur too sporadically to contribute much to the forcefulness of Donne's language.

Throughout his poetry Donne concentrates on argument and ideas. Argument is largely carried by syntax and syntactical arrangement and much of the vocabulary, particularly in the satires and lyrics, may be called syntactical. It contains a high proportion of grammatical words, such as pronouns, conjunctions, prepositions and so on.

The most essential group of grammatical words in any writing that is argument must be connectives, usually conjunctions of a reasoning kind, such as *though*; *as*; *just as*; *so*; *if*; *because*; *for* in the sense of 'because' and *yet* in the sense of 'nevertheless' or 'notwithstanding'. Donne uses these freely, often in connection with similes. An example comes from the opening of the Elegie, 'The Comparison':

> As the sweet sweat of Roses in a Still,
> As that which from chaf'd muskats pores doth trill,
> As the Almighty Balme of th'early East,
> Such are the sweat drops on my Mistris breast.
> (11.1–4)

In this series of similes there is a high proportion of monosyllables. A heavy stress also falls on *Such* at the beginning of the last line, where the initial iambic foot has been reversed. Stress is a factor in Donne's use of grammatical words and many of the quotations that follow contain examples of stress falling on lexically empty words. In 'A Valediction: forbidding Mourning' the conjunction *though* is stressed, although the strongest stress falls on the nucleus of the clause, which is *goe*. The quotation also includes the lexically empty word, *therefore*, an adverbial conjunct frequent in discourse of argument:

> Our two soules therefore, which are one,
> Though I must goe, endure not yet
> A breach, but an expansion.
> (11.21–3)

Another group of grammatical words essential to argument is

auxiliary verbs and, more particularly, modal auxiliaries. They are used profusely in the reasoning passages and often in those which contain the conjunctions already mentioned. A few lines from the Elegie, 'The Bracelet', will show the number of modals that Donne uses:

> Destin'd you *might* have been to such a one
> As *would* have lov'd and worship'd you alone,
> One which *would* suffer hunger, nakednesse,
> Yea death, ere he *would* make your number lesse;
> But I am guilty of your sad decay,
> *May* your few fellowes longer with me stay.
> (11.85–90) [my italics]

These are purely hypothetical clauses – hence the modals. There are no connectives in this passage, the argument being carried forward by modals alone. Similar examples can be found in *Songs and Sonets*.

Auxiliary verbs are often pro-forms. Many grammatical words function as 'pro-forms'; that is, they substitute for some other group, phrase or even clause. The word *pro-noun* indicates this and most people are aware that these words often represent nouns, although strictly speaking they are more likely to substitute for entire nominal groups rather than single nouns. Personal pronouns are seldom substitutions and, therefore, not usually pro-forms. Demonstrative and indefinite pronouns are pro-forms unless they are part of a nominal group. Usually pro-forms are anaphoric and refer back to the fuller form, but they can be cataphoric and refer forward to something not yet mentioned. Cataphoric reference is fairly frequent in Donne's verse.

When they occur on their own, auxiliary verbs are normally pro-forms substituting for a whole verbal group. An example comes in 'The Anniversarie':

> Two graves must hide thine and my coarse,
> If one *might*, death were no divorce.
> (11.11–12)

Might is stressed here before the caesura. The compression resulting from the pro-form makes this a typical instance of Donne's epigrammatic style. Another modal which occurs three times in one line, twice as an auxiliary and once as a pro-form, is *can* in 'Loves Alchymie'. All of these bear degrees of stress. The quotation also includes a cataphoric pro-form, *this*:

> Ends love in this, that my man,
> Can be as happy'as I can; If he can
> Endure the short scorne of a Bridegroomes play?
> (11.15–17)

Other modals appear in 'Womans Constancy':

> Vaine lunatique, against these scapes I *could*
> Dispute, and conquer, if I *would*,
> Which I abstaine to doe.
> (11.14–16) [my italics]

Could here is an ordinary modal auxiliary, but *would* is a pro-form. There is also a pro-form of the infinitive *doe*, substituting for two verbal groups.

Less striking because much more common are the modal auxiliaries *shall* and *will* used as pro-forms. Sometimes, but not often, they take a certain degree of stress because Donne places them at the end of a line. An example of the pro-form *shall* occurs in the Verse Letter 'To Sir Henry Goodyere':

> So had your body'her morning, hath her noone,
> And shall not better; her next change is night.
> (11.9–10)

Shall here substitutes for the full form *shall have*. All pro-forms must, of course, be elliptical to some extent. This is an extreme instance of the elliptical nature of Donne's writing.

Often, Donne presents an argument as a series of statements leading to an apparently logical conclusion. Poems of this type contain few modal verbs. We might, for instance, expect a poem such as 'The Flea' to have a large number of modals but, in fact, it does not because the argument progresses by statement and analogy. The relative absence of modals from the *Holy Sonnets* and other religious poems indicates that they too are poems of statement rather than of argument. In this they differ from many of Donne's love poems.

Besides modal auxiliaries Donne makes full use of primary auxiliaries. These do not necessarily forward argument but they add to the number of grammatical words in Donne's poetry. The primary auxiliaries, and particularly various forms of *be*, are frequently stressed. This is usually the outcome of syntactical inversion. Although these usages themselves do not constitute reasoning in verse, the somewhat stilted and poised effect often strengthens the impression of reasoning. An example of *be* taking stress because of inversion of complement and verb is: 'th'issue your owne ruine is' (1.27) from Satyre V, 'Thou shalt not laugh in this leafe'. There are many more instances. An example of a pro-form comes in a Verse Letter 'To Mr R.W.':

> Kindly'I envy thy Songs perfection
> Built of all th'elements as our bodyes are.
> (11.1–2)

Are implies the whole clause: 'are built of all th'elements'. Examples of auxiliary *have* as a pro-form are fewer. The use of *do* as an empty auxiliary in statements had just passed its peak in the late sixteenth century but it still occurred and was readily available for metrical convenience. Conversely, *do* in questions and negative statements, obligatory now, was still developing and Donne often omits the auxiliary in clauses of this type. *Do* and its various parts appear frequently as pro-forms. Two examples occur in one line in 'A Valediction: forbidding Mourning':

> If they be two, they are two so
>   As stiffe twin compasses are two,
> Thy soule the fixt foot, makes no show
> To move, but doth, if the'other doe.
> (11.25–8)

All primary auxiliary verbs: *be*; *have* and *do* have lexically full equivalents. 'The Sunne Rising' has two distinct uses of *is* in two consecutive lines:

> She'is all States, and all Princes, I,
>   Nothing else is.
> (11.21–2)

The first instance is a copular verb. The second, the last word of the quotation, is a form of *be* used in its lexically full sense of 'being'. The verb *be* is the only one to have virtually three functions and meanings: as an auxiliary, as a copular verb and with the lexically full form meaning 'to exist'. There are naturally many examples of *have* as a lexically full relational verb in the sense of possession. One, involving inversion and consequently taking stress, comes in 'The Dampe':

> if you dare be brave,
> And pleasure in your conquest have,
> First kill th'enormous Gyant, your *Disdaine*.
> (11.9–11)

The inversion is caused partly by the need for *have* as a rhyming word, which places it at the end of the line and also thrusts it further into prominence because it reads and sounds awkwardly. Finally, *do* in its sense of 'act' or 'perform' is found in 'The Computation':

> For the first twenty yeares, since yesterday,
> I scarce beleev'd, thou could'st be gone away,
> ...
> A thousand, I did neither thinke, nor doe.
> (11.1–2; 6)

In all these examples stress falls on the verb, usually because it is at the end of a line, or because it comes in mid-line before the caesura or, sometimes, before a syntactical break. Attention is thus drawn to the verbs, which are given unusual semantic weight.

The same verb forms often occur in stressed positions whether they are auxiliaries or lexically full verbs. Care is needed, therefore, when drawing a distinction between meaning and function, but for purposes of identifying syntactical words that are stressed the difference is unimportant.

Apart from auxiliaries, Donne uses many types of stative verb which are less lexically full than dynamic ones. Cognitive verbs, such as *know*; *think*; *dream*; *believe* and, especially, *love* occur frequently as do verbs of inert perception, such as *see*; *feel* (in its

tactile sense) and *taste*. Other non-dynamic or stative verbs are the group known as relational. Examples of these are *be*; *seem*; *feel*; *need*; *have* (in the sense of 'possess'); *involve*; *inhere* and *allow* (meaning 'grant' or 'concede').
Pronouns of various types probably form the largest single group of grammatical words that Donne uses. In this he differs from other metaphysical poets. The most obvious are personal pronouns. As noted earlier, these are not usually pro-forms. As we should expect, the most frequent pronoun is the first person singular *I* but the inclusive plural *we* also occurs frequently in the love poetry. Donne is intensely preoccupied with love relationships. Unlike his courtly predecessors, who addressed their mistresses from a distance, he explores the mutual emotions of lover and beloved and this necessitates the use of the inclusive pronoun. Examples of personal pronouns are:

> neglected thou
> Bath'd in a cold quicksilver sweat wilt lye
>   A veryer ghost then I;
>   (' The Apparition' 11.11–13)

and:

> Alas, as well as other Princes, wee,
> (Who Prince enough in one another bee,)
> Must leave at last in death ...
>   ('The Anniversarie' 11.13–15)

The pronouns in these quotations fall at the ends of lines and, even when the line is run on, as in line 11 of the first example, take some degree of metrical stress. The reader is conscious of the slight pause that adds to the emphasis. An instance of the inclusive plural *we* in oblique form occurs in 'The Canonization':

> all shall approve
> Us *Canoniz'd* for Love.
>   (11.35–6)

The pronoun *Us* comes at the beginning of the line but again it is stressed syntactically because it is the head of the complement group (a single word in this case) that ends the clause. This time the metrical foot is not inverted as the first syllable of the following word is also stressed. An example with two consecutive stressed pronouns comes from one of the *Holy Sonnets*: 'Wilt thou love God, as he thee!' Donne frequently stresses juxtaposed syllables and this is one reason for the disjointed or harsh-sounding impression made by his verse.

Demonstrative pronouns, *this*; *that* and their equivalent plurals, *these* and *those*, are, unlike the personal pronouns, frequently pro-forms. They, or the possessive forms of the personal pronouns, preclude articles, since they are mutually exclusive. Articles, definite or indefinite, are used sparingly in Donne's verse. 'The Anniversarie' affords examples of demonstrative pronouns functioning as pro-forms:

> Only our love hath no decay;
> This, no tomorrow hath, nor yesterday;
> (11.7–8)

and:

> But soules where nothing dwells but love
> (All other thoughts being inmates) then shall prove
> This, or a love increased there above.
> (11.17–19)

This – for different reasons – is stressed on both occasions. In the first example it is not only the first word and the subject of its clause but is followed by a pause. The pause is even more marked than it might be because the expected order of the verb and complement following has been reversed. Here, we see again syntactical stress thrown by inversion on to the relational verb *hath*. In the second example *This* is the final word of the clause, the point towards which the argument has been working. It refers forward cataphorically to a proposition stated in the following line:

> When bodies to their graves, soules from their
>   graves remove.
> (1.20)

Related to the demonstrative pronouns is the definite pronoun *such*. It also functions as a pro-form. An instance was seen earlier in the Elegie, 'The Comparison' (p.25):

> Such are the sweat drops on my Mistris breast.
> (1.4)

Most of the wide-ranging group of indefinite pronouns occur many times. The group includes *some*; *something*; *nothing*; *every*; *each*; *one*; *none*; *no* and, predominant in its frequency, *all*. These pronouns, too, with the notable exceptions of *all* and *nothing*, are usually pro-forms. Examples of indefinite pronouns are *none* in 'The Broken Heart':

> I brought a heart into the roome,
> But from the roome, I carried none with mee;
> (11.19–20)

and *one* in 'Hymn to God my God, in my sicknesse', with word play typical of Donne:

> As West and East
> In all flatt Maps (and I am one) are one,
> So death doth touch the Resurrection.
> (11.13–15)

The first *one* is a pronoun and also functions as a pro-form for 'all flatt Maps'. The second instance is a cardinal number. In these examples, again, the pronouns are stressed, as is the preposition *from*, contrasting with *into* in the first quotation. An extract from the Verse Letter *To Sir Edward Herbert, at Julyers*, which contains numerous instances of *all*, usually as a pronoun but once as a predeterminer, is:

> for Man into himselfe can draw
> All; All his faith can swallow,'or reason chaw.
> All that is fill'd, and all that which doth fill,
> All the round world, to man is but a pill;
> In all it workes not, but it is in all
> Poysonous, or purgative, or cordiall.
> (11.37–42)

Every one of the six instances of the pronoun and the predeterminer takes some degree of stress. None, however, is a pro-form.

Besides the pronouns already mentioned, there is the *wh-* group, which includes relatives and interrogatives. Interrogatives are the most common. Such words as *who* and *what* used in an absolute sense also occur. In 'Aire and Angels' we find:

> And therefore what thou wert, and who,
>   I bid Love aske.
> (11.11–12)

The interrogatives here balance the two *wh-* words, only one a pronoun, from earlier in the poem:

> Still when, to where thou wert, I came.
> (1.5)

In 'Elegie on Prince Henry' there is an even longer string of these words, used in a similar way:

> Where, how, when, what, soules do departed hence:
> These things (eccentrique else) on Faith do strike.
> (11.12–13)

The sequence of interrogative words is typical of the Jesuitical method of questioning, not only existence itself, with which Donne was much concerned, but also the precise nature of that existence. *Do* in the first line is an example of the lexically full use of the verb. Donne occasionally uses a compound form: *whoever* or *whatever*, and also the compounds *nowhere* and *anywhere*. Once, at least, he resorts to functional shift to make one of these a noun in 'The Good-Morrow':

> For love, all love of other sights controules,
>   And makes one little roome, an every where.
> (11.10–11)

The use of so many grammatical words brings us to a problem that is central in Donne's poetry. How, if he relies so heavily on grammatical and lexically empty words, do the poems give the palpable impression of being full of energy and meaning? This seems to contradict the argument posited earlier, when examining borrowed words, that abstract vocabulary dissipates energy. Paradoxically, although no one could deny that some of the energy, at least, derives from the fantastic conceits and their associated vocabulary, Donne achieves much of his peculiar forcefulness through these very grammatical words. This is partly brought about by the way in which he contrives to make stress fall in unexpected ways on grammatical words, especially those functioning as pro-forms. This we have seen. Syntactical arrangement is an additional factor and has also been commented on incidentally in analysing the use of grammatical words.

Syntax and metre both provide answers to this question. The two are inextricably interwoven. Donne was himself the first to call his verse 'harsh', an epithet that others have since applied to it. In one of the *Verse Letters*, 'To Mr T. W.', he begins:

> Hast [haste] thee harsh verse, as fast as thy lame measure
> Will give thee leave,
>
> (11.1–2)

and in the one 'To Mr S. B.' he says:

> I sing not, Siren-like, to tempt; for I
> Am harsh.
>
> (11.9–10)

Donne equates harshness with the metre or 'measure' he uses, but the clause arrangement also adds to the apparent abruptness, especially in the love poetry. Most clauses in *Songs and Sonets* are short. The complement and verb elements are sometimes inverted, giving the order S C V. Very often this throws stress and end focus on to a grammatical verb such as *be*, *have* or even *do* and this creates syntactical dislocation. There are relatively few embedded postmodifying clauses, either as part of complements, the most usual place, or of subjects. Interpolated clauses and phrases placed out of normal order, however, occur frequently. This is also true of the *Holy Sonnets*, although the clauses are often slightly longer. On the whole, the *Verse Letters* follow normal word and group order more closely, as do the

Anniversaries. The *Anniversaries*, however, have longer and more intricately composed clause complexes.

In *Songs and Sonets* the clauses usually fall into the space of a single line or just run on into the next. This preponderance of short clauses, sometimes broken by interposed clauses, with few long nominal groups, tends to create an abrupt jerky rhythm, especially when the syntactical stress does not coincide with the metrical stress. This abruptness is further emphasized by run-on lines with the clause ending at the caesura of the next line or, very often, before it. The latter, especially, makes for the harshness of which Donne speaks. It also helps to give the verse its vigorous quality and is often equated with an assumption that Donne adopts the rhythms of speech. The differing lengths of line also contribute to the unevenness of metre and reinforce this assumption. A line of five or four feet is sometimes followed by one of only two. An example of this from 'Womans Constancy' is:

> Now thou hast lov'd me one whole day,
> To morrow when thou leav'st, what wilt thou say?
> Wilt thou then Antedate some new made vow?
>   Or say that now
> We are not just those persons, which we were?
> (11.1–5)

The first line has four feet, the second, third and fifth have five with the fourth having only two. The second line is broken into two parts, the first of three feet and the second, which contains the main clause, of two. The fourth short line runs on to the following five-foot line, although there is a clear pause for the ear after *now*, partly because of the rhyme with *vow*, which ends the preceding line. The next example is from 'Loves Usury':

> For every hour that thou wilt spare mee now,
>   I will allow
> Usurious God of Love, twenty to thee.
> (11.1–3)

The norm is again a five-foot line and here, in the first line, metrical stress coincides with syntactical stress. Again the short line runs over into the next but the complement of the verb *allow* – which rhymes with the line before – is deferred by the interpolated vocative phrase. Both of these examples come from the openings of poems, before the complex metrical pattern of the whole poem is established. Later, the short lines are less surprising.

At the beginning of poems, too, we seem to hear something like a speaking voice. The abrupt openings, particularly those in the form of direct address, are the main reason for the widespread supposition that Donne's verse is speech-based. Some of the best-known openings of *Songs and Sonets* are particularly vigorous:

> Busie old foole, unruly Sunne,
> Why dost thou thus,
> Through windowes, and through curtaines call on us?
> ('The Sunne Rising' 11.1–3)

and:

> For Godsake hold your tongue, and let me love.
> ('The Canonization' 1.1)

These, of course, are not actual speech. The impression is illusory and derives chiefly from the often rough openings of address, followed by Donne's abrupt-seeming clause structure and compressed style.

There is much ellipsis, often involving the use of pro-forms. Sometimes it is straightforward but when complex it can become ambiguous. In either case the compression that results helps to account for a sense of energy in the verse. One of the *Holy Sonnets* provides an instance:

> Since she whome I lovd, hath payd her last debt
> To Nature, and to hers, and my good is dead ....
> (11.1–2)

The ellipsis comes in the use of the independent possessive form of the pronoun *hers*, which implies *her* + noun. The difficulty is to identify which noun in the text is implied – *Nature* or *good*.

The meaning could be that the woman has paid the debt due to her own 'nature' as well as to the natural order of the physical world – *Nature*. Her 'nature' is mortal and as a consequence she must die. The parallelism of the structures *To Nature* and *to hers* makes this seem the likely interpretation, except that *Nature* is not a possessive and therefore is not grammatically identical with *hers*. It also requires a semantic shift, the word *Nature* being used in two related but slightly different senses. The other possible noun implied in *hers* is *good*: 'she is dead to her own good as well as to mine'. The possessive forms of *hers* and *my good* balance but the punctuation and the omission of *to* before *my good* obscure the connection. Both nouns may be included in the reference of the pro-form with an intentional ambiguity. Another example from the same sonnet is:

> But why shoud I begg more love, when as thou
> Dost wooe my soule, for hers offring all thine?
> (11.9–10)

These two lines are even more obscure because of the independent personal pronouns in the final clause. *Thine*, which refers to God, and *hers* present the same type of problem as *hers* in the previous quotation. The nouns implied must be either *love* or *soule*, but which is intended in either case is far from clear and becomes less so as one attempts to unravel the meaning. Out of nineteen words only five are lexically full. The grammatical words shed all impression of emptiness; first because they are stressed and then because of the compressed meaning. An example of complex syntax, which involves both ellipsis and substitution, comes at the end of *The Second Anniversarie,*:

> nor wouldst thou be content,
> To take this, for my second yeeres true Rent,
> Did this Coine bear any'other stampe, then his
> That gave thee power to doe, me, to say this.
> (11.519–22)

The ellipses in the final line arise from the use of pro-forms of various types.

Donne frequently uses resumption to extend the rather longer sentences, particularly in the *Anniversaries*. This results in parallel constructions of the type: 'She, for whose losse ... (12 lines); But she, in whom ... (2 lines); She, from whose influence ... (10 lines); She that did thus ... (2 lines)' (*The First Anniversarie*, 11.401–26). Another example is 'Shee, who ... (2 lines); Who ... (4 lines); Who ... (4 lines); Who ... (2 lines); Who ... (2 lines); Whose ... (1 line); Who ... (1 line); Who ... (3 lines); ... shee to heaven is gone,/Who made ... (3 lines)' (*The Second Anniversarie*, 11.449–70).

Metre and syntax, including ellipsis, therefore, contribute to the vigorous quality of Donne's use of language as well as to compression of meaning. Although sentences can be lengthy, as in the *Anniversaries*, it is not length that necessarily makes for complexity. Indeed, the energy is evident less in these poems than in the shorter lyrics, in which the metre is more varied. A final brief example from *Songs and Sonets*, composed entirely of short lines and clauses, shows many of Donne's typical syntactic and metrical features. It comes at the beginning of 'The Paradox':

> No Lover saith, I love, nor any other
> Can judge a perfect Lover;
> Hee thinkes that else none can nor will agree,
> That any loves but hee.
> (11.1–4)

Altogether there are seven clauses in these four lines, three in the first semantic unit and the rest, in the second, mainly made up of reported clauses after the verbs *think* and *agree*. The third line contains ellipsis and it is here that the reader becomes confused about the meaning. As in the previous cases of ellipsis, the punctuation seems to impede the sense rather than help to make it clear. The composition of the clause throws the auxiliaries *can* and *will* into prominence. Because of their opposition in meaning and syntax they are both stressed even more strongly than their ordinary stressed position would demand. It is in ways such as these that Donne creates the forcefulness associated with his poetry.

Besides the preponderance of grammatical words, which are basically abstract, Donne does use concrete images and vocabulary. This is very obvious in his daring and unusual metaphors and similes, many of them incorporating hyperbole. This aspect of his writing is so well-known that a few examples will be sufficient to show his use of concrete and often visual images or conceits. Metaphors are used as intellectual links between the image and the object which the speaker has in view. A clear example is 'The Flea'. In this poem, Donne uses one image throughout. The argument whereby the flea mingles the blood of the lovers and constitutes their 'marriage bed' is purely intellectual and casuistical but the end of the argument is physical seduction. Similarly, 'A Valediction: of Weeping' contains the image of the Elizabethan conception of the globe, with its three continents:[6]

> On a round ball
> A workeman that hath copies by, can lay
> An Europe, Afrique, and an Asia,
> And quickly make that, which was nothing, *All*.
>
> (11.10–13)

The image is used only for purposes of reasoning: the tears of the lover's mistress are globes, each of which bears her likeness and which, mingling with his own tears, drown the world and result in destroying his heaven, that is his earthly happiness in their love:

> So doth each teare,
> Which thee doth weare,
> A globe, yea world by that impression grow,
> Till thy teares mixt with mine doe overflow
> This world, by waters sent from thee, my heaven
> dissolved so.
>
> (11.14–17)

Donne here uses hyperbole. It is not unlike Crashaw's images involving tears, notably those in 'The Weeper'.

Images in the *Holy Sonnets* and *Hymns* are usually physical. 'Hymne to God my God, in my sicknesse' uses the image of a map to represent the body of the dying man, examined by the 'cosmographers', the doctors:

> Whilst my Physitians by their love are growne
>   Cosmographers, and I their Mapp, who lie
> Flat on this bed.
>
> (11.6–8)

There is no intellectual argument in these images. Even the ultimate dissolution of death, which liberates the soul from the body, is at least a partly physical experience and the geographical (and topical) images are sustained:

> this is my South-west discoverie
> *Per fretum febris*, by these streights to die.
> (11.9–10)

The images used in the examples cited are almost all emblematic. They are visual but not in a representational way. Tears, globes and maps were conventional emblems. In one of the *Holy Sonnets* Donne combines the idea of the globe with the long outmoded notion of a flat world:

> At the round earths imagin'd corners, blow
> Your trumpets, Angells ...
> (11.1–2)

It is the emblem tradition that allows Donne to present these two world views visually and simultaneously, one superimposed upon the other.[7] Another typical emblem is the storm-tossed ship that Donne uses in 'The Storme', and also in 'A Hymne to Christ, at the Authors last going into Germany'. In this poem Donne actually uses the word *embleme*:

> In what torne ship soever I embarke,
> That ship shall be my embleme of thy Arke;
> What sea soever swallow mee, that flood
> Shall be to mee an embleme of thy blood.
> (11.1–4)

The ship in a storm is a Petrarchan image (originally derived from Ovid) but it became part of the emblem tradition. A similar example is that of the licking of bear cubs in the Elegie, 'Loves Progress':

> And love's a beare-whelpe borne; if wee'over-licke
> Our love, and force it new strange shapes to take
> We erre, and of a lumpe a monster make.
> (11.4–6)

Mythology held that bear cubs were born amorphous lumps that were licked into shape by their mothers. Donne twists the emblem to suit his own argument. He frequently loosens or extends the application of a traditional emblem.

Sometimes, the images show the influence of the Jesuit emblem tradition. In the Holy Sonnet, 'Batter my heart', the poet implores God to chastise him with the various types of suffering that were illustrated in those emblems in which hearts were drawn with hands hammering them, piercing them with nails and other tortures. Another instance from the Holy Sonnets, 'Thou hast made me', embodies the narrative idiom present in Francis Quarles's emblems, which depict the religious adventures of *Anima* (the Soul):

> I runne to death, and death meets me as fast,
> And all my pleasures are like yesterday,
> I dare not move my dimme eyes any way,
> Despaire behind and death before doth cast
> Such terrour ...
> (11.3–7)

Similar is the image of man toiling towards truth in Satyre III, 'Kinde pitty chokes my spleene':

> On a huge hill,
> Cragged, and steep, Truth stands, and hee that will
> Reach her, about must, and about must goe.
> (11.79–81)

Knowledge of the emblem tradition helps the reader to understand the strange pictorial quality that Donne often draws, as in the Holy Sonnet, 'I am a little world':

> Powre new seas in mine eyes, that so I might
> Drowne my world with my weeping earnestly.
> (11.7–8)

The picture this image conjures up could easily appear in an emblem, grotesque as it is.[8] To be able to visualize the type of emblematic illustration that might accompany this is to come closer to understanding not only what the image is but also the meaning it is intended to convey within the poem. It is similar to several of Crashaw's more extravagant images in 'The Weeper'.

In many poems Donne uses conventional metaphors and similes that do not draw attention to themselves. These show that he could equally well handle traditional poetic imagery. His more startling conceits occur in clusters and only then in some poems. They are more widely scattered than the repeated references to them by commentators suggest. Critics pay attention to them because they are striking in themselves and often unpoetic within the lyric convention. It is the sporadic occurrence of such images in Donne's poetry that gives them their forcefulness and makes them easy to extract for examination. Such images do not so much make straight comparisons as draw the reader's attention to correspondences. The notion of correspondences as an essential part of the cosmos, including life on this planet, was one of the most important preoccupations of Elizabethan thought.[9] Some poems rely on different types of rhetoric to give the verse its sense of energy.

Perhaps the principal rhetorical device that Donne uses, apart from conceits and emblems, is repetition in all its many forms. In common with his contemporaries, he rang the changes on all the various effects these allowed: riddling, paradox, punning and so forth. The favourite kind of repetition was of individual words. Many different figures of this type were distinguished in Elizabethan rhetoric and Donne used most of them at one time or another. Sister Miriam Joseph notes that:

> the figures of repetition in addition to pleasing the ear have the functional value of emphasizing ideas and the movement of thought ... [10]

This 'functional value' is central to Donne's patterns of repetition. No slavish follower of habit, he frequently moves away from the set rules of the manuals of rhetoric and adapts the figures of repetition to assist that 'movement of thought' which is essential to his own kind of poetry.

Grammatical or lexically empty words are often repeated and acquire a force and significance that they would not otherwise have. Examples have already been given. The most commonly repeated words of this type, apart from forms of the verb *be*, are the indefinite pronouns *all* and *none* or *nothing*. They are contrasted and equated in a Verse Letter 'To the Countesse of Huntington': 'As all things were one nothing' (1.37). Another example, with a paradoxical and chiastic inversion of the clause elements in the second line which results in epigram, occurs in 'To the Countesse of Bedford' ('T'have written then'):

> ... *nothings*, as I am, may
> Pay all they have, and yet have all to pay.
> (11.7–8)

This incorporates the figure of *antimetabole*. An instance of word play on *all* and a derivative word (another kind of verbal repetition common in Donne: *polyptoton*) is found in 'A Letter to the Lady Carey, and Mrs Essex Riche': 'True vertue'is *Soule*, Alwaies in all deeds *All*.' (1.36). An example of *all* repeated through a passage was quoted earlier from the Verse Letter *To Sir Edward Herbert, at Julyers* (p.32). The beginning of the Verse Letter 'To the Lady Bedford' contains an instance of Donne's riddling verbal play and repeats many grammatical words:

> You that are she and you, that's double shee,
> In her dead face, halfe of your selfe shall see;
> Shee was the other part, for so they doe
> Which build them friendships, become one of two.
> (11.1–4)

This type of intricate epigrammatic writing is more typical of *Songs and Sonets*.[11] Lexically full words, particularly certain key words such as *love*, are also repeated in various patterns. Occasionally words, or a word, are repeated throughout an entire passage, as in *The Second Anniversarie*, the elegiac poem on the death of Elizabeth Drury:

> shee to Heaven is gone,
> Who made this world in some proportion
> A heaven, and here, became unto us all,
> Joye, (as our joyes admit) essentiall.
> But could this low world joyes essentiall touch,
> Heavens accidentall joyes would passe them much.
> (11.467–72)

The words *joy*; *heaven*; *world*; *essentiall*; *accidentall* and also *casuall* occur throughout much of the poem, subtitled 'The Progress of the Soule'. They are central to its meaning. In the lines quoted, the contrast between 'heaven' and the 'world' is emphasized by repetition. The repetition of *essentiall* is also important, since it literally implies the 'essence' of the joy of the soul of the dead girl as she is received into heaven. This in turn contrasts with the *accidentall* joys of heaven, which far surpass any earthly conception of 'essentiall' and everlasting joy.

A different kind of repetition is that in which Donne repeats not the word itself but the part of speech. He does this occasionally with nouns, as in the Holy Sonnet, 'At the round earths imagined corners', in which, at the Day of Judgement, the angel's trumpets summon:

    All whom the flood did, and fire shall o'erthrow,
    All whom warre, dearth, age, agues, tyrannies,
    Despaire, law, chance, hath slain ...
                             (11.5–7)

In this example the lines gather momentum in a way that reflects the pouring forth of the dead souls. In the first line stress falls on the auxiliary verb *did*, another instance of the syntactic dislocation that creates the abruptness and feeling of energy in Donne's verse. The reference here is cataphoric, which pushes the reader forward and adds to the sense of urgency conveyed in these lines. Donne also uses strings of dynamic verbs. One such sequence is found in the Elegie, 'On his Mistris' (note the heavily stressed *I* repeated at the end of the first line):

    I saw him, I,
    Assayld, fight, taken, stabb'd, bleede, fall, and dye.
                              (11.53–4)

The same thing is found in the Holy Sonnet, 'Batter my heart':

                      for, you
    As yet but knocke, breathe, shine, and seeke to mend;
    That I may rise, and stand, o'erthrow mee,'and bend
    Your force, to breake, blowe, burn and make me new.
                              (11.1–4)

The last three lines are composed almost entirely of verbs. There are thirteen (not counting the modal auxiliary *may*) and, whatever their form, they are all dynamic. This adds significantly to the vigorous quality of the verse, particularly in the final line in which each verb takes stress.

The paradoxical and riddling elements in Donne's verse make for close-packed meaning, which in turn is another source of energy. Frequently the expression is epigrammatically terse. An instance of extreme paradox, the final couplet of which is also an epigram, occurs at the end of the sonnet just quoted:

> Take mee to you, imprison mee, for I
> Except you'enthrall mee, never shall be free,
> Nor ever chast, except you ravish me.
> (11.1–4)

Another example involves *antimetabole*. The whole proposition is repeated in reverse order in the last line of the poem. The two lines quoted refer to the creation of Adam and the birth of Christ, although neither is named:

> 'Twas much, that man was made like God before,
> But, that God should be made like man, much more.
> ('Wilt thou love God' 11.13–14)

Paradox occurs earlier in this sonnet:

> Oh, to vex me, contraryes meete in one:
> Inconstancy unnaturally hath begott
> A constant habit; that when I would not
> I change in vowes, and in devotione.
> (11.1–4)

Here is another instance of *polyptoton* (the repetition of a word in a different form): *Inconstancy* and *constant*. The whole poem is constructed round opposites, both words and concepts: *constant habit* and *change*; *cold* and *hott*; *praying* and *mute*; *infinit* and *none*. It ends with the final paradox of seeming disease being a state of true health:

> So my devout fitts come and go away
> Like a fantastique Ague: save that here
> Those are my best dayes, when I shake with feare.
> (11.12–14)

Besides being a common feature of poetry at the time, Donne's riddling was partly a natural outcome of his Roman Catholic upbringing and education. It would have been further encouraged by any Elizabethan Grammar School. Another instance of paradox comes from 'Goodfriday, 1613. Riding Westward':

> Hence is't, that I am carryed towards the West
> This day, when my Soules forme bends toward the East.
> There I should see a Sunne, by rising set,
> And by that setting endlesse day beget.
> (11.9–12)

The juxtaposition of *set* and *setting* (*polyptoton*) draws attention to the paradox.

Much of Donne's forcefulness derives from the way in which he uses images and rhetoric. In these areas, and particularly in the various types of repetition, he uses grammatical words as well as others of a more concrete kind. There is a consistency about his language that is often missed because certain aspects of it have engaged attention to the neglect of others. His language is ratiocinative and he argues through his vocabulary, syntax and images, forcing the reader to use powers of reasoning to reach the meaning. Imagination, which we associate with much of the poetry we know best, is not absent from Donne's verse. Instead of working through the senses, however, it requires a deliberate effort of mind to connect the ideas and the vehicle by which they are conveyed.

3 George Herbert (1593–1633)

> *'all good structure'*
> 'Jordan' (I)

Unlike Donne, Herbert has one theme only and it runs through all his writings: Christianity and Christian experience. Inevitably much of his vocabulary is taken from religious sources, principally the Bible, but also the Liturgy and other medieval and Renaissance works and devotional writings, not excluding religious lyrics and the illuminated Books of Hours. Two well-known and popular books were the *Biblia Pauperum* and the *Speculum humanae salvationis*, both of which were illustrated.[1] Herbert uses these not so much for vocabulary as for the inter-relating of images and symbols, and thus enriches the significance of many biblical allusions. References to the Bible and biblical stories of the Old and New Testaments are common. Often Herbert simply uses the names of biblical characters, clearly expecting his readers to be familiar with the context and significance of the names. An example is in the first stanza of 'Decay':

> Sweet were the dayes, when thou didst lodge with Lot,
> Struggle with Jacob, sit with Gideon,
> Advise with Abraham, when thy power could not
> Encounter Moses strong complaints and mone:
>   Thy words were then, *Let me alone*.
>
>   (11.1–5)

The final words are taken from Exodus XXXII.10. Frequently,

Herbert mixes allusions to the Old and New Testaments so that the meaning of the New Testament gains in depth by the cross-reference. This is firmly in the tradition of both the New Testament itself and Church teaching. One instance of this intermingling of symbolic vocabulary comes in 'The Bunch of Grapes':

> But can he want the grape, who hath the wine?
> I have their fruit and more.
> Blessed be God, who prosper'd *Noah's* vine,
>   And made it bring forth grapes good store.
>   But much more him I must adore,
> Who of the Laws sowre juice sweet wine did make,
> Ev'n God himself being pressed for my sake.
>   (11.22–8)

The set of words to do with vines and wine-making: *grape*; *wine*; *vine* and *pressed* is found throughout both the Old and New Testaments. The allusion to '*Noah's* vine' (Genesis IX.20) may be unfamiliar to readers nowadays but the image of Christ as the 'true vine', from whom comes the life-giving blood or wine of the sacrament, is a traditional one. Herbert emphasizes the events of the New rather than the Old Testament, especially the birth, crucifixion and resurrection of Christ. In these the vocabulary is less directly biblical, although still related to the event, as in 'Christmas':

> O Thou, whose glorious, yet contracted light,
>   Wrapt in nights mantle, stole into a manger.
>   (11. 9–10)

Only *manger* is a strictly biblical word but the others, collocating with it, take on a religious significance. Sometimes the title of a poem is simply a biblical text, as 'Ephesians iv. 30: *Grieve not the Holy Spirit, &c.*'

Besides biblical vocabulary, and names and allusions incorporating words taken from religion, there are frequent references to the Church itself, both to its buildings and to its festive seasons. *The Temple* begins with a poem which is clearly intended as the entry to the Church: 'The Church-Porch'. Later we have 'Church-musick'; 'Church-lock and key'; 'The Church-floore' and so on. Then there are various titles referring to Church services: 'Holy Baptisme'; 'The Holy Communion' and 'Even-song', and festal days, such as 'Easter' and 'Whitsunday'. The activities of the Church are named in such titles as 'Prayer'; 'The Thanksgiving' and 'Confession'.

Apart from the ever-present religious vocabulary, one of Herbert's chief sources of words – and the one which he uses most in his imagery – is everyday domestic life. Unlike Donne, who looked outwards to the wider world and beyond to the heavens and cosmos, Herbert seems to reverse the process and locates the vastness of the mystery of religion in everyday objects around him. Instead of using a telescope he prefers a microscope. Much household vocabulary relates to the country or town house. In 'Redemption' the poet seeks Christ, his *rich Lord*, in heaven at his *manour*. In the same poem is the line: 'In cities, theatres, gardens, parks, and courts,' (1.11) which clearly indicates where Herbert's early interests lay. Words denoting various rooms, as well as other parts of houses – *stairs; floor; windows* – are all found, as are words to do with furnishing – *furniture* itself; *table; chair; bed; curtains; clock; box; chest* and *cabinet*. This is the vocabulary of the 'household-stuffe' (1.9) mentioned in 'Affliction' (I). In addition there are words to do with culinary and other domestic processes: *cinnamon; cloves; nutmeg; spice* and *pomander*. There are many references to clothing and the fabrics from which clothes are made: *clothes; cloth; linen; silks; furs; wool* and even the *taylor* who makes these into clothes, as well as the *silk twist* that he uses. Man, himself, metaphorically

> ... wears a stuffe whose thread is course and round,
> But trimm' d with curious lace.
> ('Mans medley' 11.15–16)

Music is a much worked source of metaphor. According to Izaak Walton, Herbert played the lute and viol and, while he lived at Bemerton, went twice a week to Salisbury to hear the Cathedral music. This is an area of vocabulary that is much used symbolically in the various medieval and Renaissance writings that Herbert drew upon for his imagery.

When he ventures to take words from outdoor life, Herbert mostly limits himself to the formal garden. His love of order out of doors as well as in is shown by an image from 'The Familie':

> First Peace and Silence all disputes controll,
>   Then Order plaies the soul;
> And giving all things their set forms and houres,
>   Makes of wilde woods sweet walks and bowres.
>
>   (11.9–12)

Other words relating to gardens are *rose*; *fine grass*; *bees*; *herbs*; *peacock*; *posy*; *blossom* and the word *garden* itself, in 'Gods rich garden'. Occasionally, he mentions a flower name: *the Crown Imperiall* and *All-heal*. Both of these can be found in Herbals of the time and apparently grew near London or in London gardens.[2] The orderly tenor of his outdoor vocabulary, so unlike the wild grandeur of the Romantics or even the simple uncultivated nature of Vaughan, is summed up in two lines from 'Vertue':

> Sweet spring, full of sweet dayes and roses,
> A box where sweets compacted lie.
>
>   (11.9–11)

Another group of words comes, perhaps surprisingly, from trade and commerce. These are also found in the poetry of Donne and appear, too, in that of Crashaw and Vaughan. *Trade*; *commerce*; *wares*; *purchase*; *profits*; *weigh* are some examples. Although few compared with other types of words mentioned and scattered through the verse, they usually come in clusters, making a consistent set of images through a single poem or part of a poem. An example is found in 'The Pearl':

> I flie to thee, and fully understand
> Both the main sale, and the commodities;
> And at what rate and price I have thy love.
>
>   (11.33–5)

Another occurs in 'The Odour', which Herbert calls 'This breathing':

> This breathing would with gains by sweetning me
>   (As sweet things traffick when they meet)
>   Return to thee.
> And so this new commerce and sweet
> Should all my life employ, and busie me.
>
>   (11.26–30)

Other smaller groups of words come from the sea and warfare, and a few from sport, including bowls, and other occupations and interests of Jacobean England, such as alchemy and some aspects of the science that fascinated Donne. But Herbert looks chiefly to town life for his vocabulary and imagery. Various trades and occupations are mentioned or can be inferred from words associated with them. One is gardening, from which come the words *pruning-knife*; *watring pots* and *gardener*. Stonemasonry occurs in 'The Altar' and 'Nature':

> O smooth my rugged heart, and there
> Engrave thy rev'rend Law and fear;
> Or make a new one, since the old
>   Is saplesse grown,
>   And a much fitter stone
> To hide my dust, then thee to hold;
>   (11.13–18)

carpentry in 'Confession':

> No scrue, no piercer can
> Into a piece of timber work and winde;
>   (11.7–8)

clock mending briefly in 'Even-song':

> And give new wheels to our disorder'd clocks;
>   (1.24)

and stained-glass work in 'The Windows':

> But when thou dost anneal in glasse thy storie,
>   Making thy life to shine within
> The holy Preachers; then the light and glorie
>   More rev'rend grows ...
>   (11.6–9)

Anneal is a technical term used for the process of fixing the colours in stained glass and it occurs more than once in the poems.

Most of the words cited to exemplify Herbert's sources of vocabulary so far have been nouns and these most readily demonstrate the areas on which he draws. Herbert uses nouns and verbs in about the same ratio but the verbs, while equally concrete, are often less specific to the subject than the nouns. When dealing with trades, which are essentially activities involving verbs, it was necessary to quote short extracts. Neither *work* nor *winde* from the extract on carpentry would obviously be associated with the craft out of context. Very many nouns and verbs are concrete, although abstract nouns denoting emotions, and particularly related to religious contemplation, are also frequent. The relative sparseness of adjectives is the result of Herbert's verse being, as Donne's, intellectual rather than descriptive. Such adjectives as he uses are often commonplace: *new*; *good*; *fine*, interspersed with a few more striking ones: '*brittle crazie* glasse' ('The Windows', 1.2); 'a *ruffling* winde' ('Constancie', 1.7) and a few compounds, such as '*Christ-side-piercing* spear' ('Prayer' (I), 1.6). Favourite adjectives are *trim* and *neat* and the ubiquitous *sweet*.

Whereas Donne's religious verse often deals with theology, Herbert's is practical and mostly has a concrete starting point. Thus his titles are frequently emblematic: 'The Pulley'; 'The Collar' and 'The Bag'. These emblems are themselves a form of riddle, both concealing and indicating the subject of the poems that follow; their significance becomes plain only after the poem has been read. 'The Pulley' deals with man's relation to God and God's device to draw his creature to him:

> When God at first made man,
> Having a glasse of blessings standing by;
> Let us (said he) poure on him all we can;
>
> (11.1–3)

but seeing *rest* lying in the bottom, he decides to withhold this final blessing:

> Yet let him keep the rest,
> But keep them with repining restlessnesse:
> Let him be rich and wearie, that at least,
> If goodnesse leade him not, yet wearinesse
>   May tosse him to my breast.
>
> (11.16–20)

Word play and riddling is apparent in the pun on *rest* and in the juxtaposition of *rest* and *restlessnesse* (*polyptoton*). The theme suggested by this poem is one that runs throughout the religious verse of Vaughan. 'The Collar' represents the servitude of man to God, against which man rebels. 'The Bag' is itself a highly elaborate conceit. The rent made in Christ's side by the Roman soldier's spear becomes a mailbag, through which man can send messages to God, and which Christ will guard with care since they are 'very neare my heart'. In this way, the 'bag' becomes a symbol or emblem for the very significance of the crucifixion.[3]

The relevance of the title 'Jordan' for two of the poems may escape modern readers. The River Jordan is rich in associations in both the Old and New Testaments. It was this river that the Israelites crossed to reach the Promised Land after their wanderings in the Wilderness. It also symbolizes, through Christ's baptism in its waters, the entry into everlasting life. For this reason, too, it has become a symbol of humility. When Elisha told Naaman to cure himself of leprosy by bathing in it, the Syrian leader was at first too proud to obey, declaring that there were rivers as good in his own country (II Kings V.1–14). In the 'Jordan' poems it represents Herbert's intention to adopt a plain method in his writing and to avoid the fanciful ornamental style of his predecessors:

> Who sayes that fictions onely and false hair
> Become a verse? Is there in truth no beautie?
> Is all good structure in a winding stair?
> ('Jordan' (I) 11.1–3)

> I envie no mans nightingale or spring;
> Nor let them punish me with losse of rime,
>   Who plainly say, *My God, My King.*
>   ('Jordan' (I) 11.13–15)

Herbert, however, by no means always kept to plain writing. The titles of his poems demonstrate in short score many of the features of his vocabulary and language. In spite of their apparent homeliness, the frequent emblematic nature of many, as well as their sources in religious observances and the Bible, is evidence of the symbolic and metaphorical type of writing that characterizes his linguistic habits.

Like Donne's, many of Herbert's clauses take up the length of a line, but because many lines are short he has a great number of very short clauses. Two stanzas from 'Businesse' illustrate this:

> If he had not liv'd for thee,
> Thou hadst di'd most wretchedly;
> And two deaths had been thy fee.
>
> He so farre thy good did plot,
> That his own self he forgot.
> Did he die, or did he not?
> (11.20-5)

No clause here is longer than a line and the last line of the second stanza has two clauses, the second containing ellipsis. Not all clauses are contained within one line. A poem in which Herbert has many run-on lines is 'Complaining'. The first two stanzas are:

> Do not beguile my heart,
> Because thou art
> My power and wisdome. Put me not to shame,
> Because I am
> Thy clay that weeps, thy dust that calls.
>
> Thou art the Lord of glorie;
> The deed and storie
> Are both thy due: but I a silly flie,
> That live or die
> According as the weather falls.
> (11.1-10)

Here we have an unusual rhyme scheme: the final word of the first stanza is not matched until the end of the second. The second clause of the first stanza runs into the third line and is followed by a very short imperative clause. The clause that begins in the fourth line is concluded in the final line, and the stanza ends with another very short clause. The second stanza follows a similar pattern, although in the clause at the end of the third line the verb is ellipted. The fourth line contains two clauses and the fifth line has one. 'Bitter-sweet' contains, perhaps more clauses per line than most poems. It consists of only two stanzas:

> Ah my deare angrie Lord,
> Since thou dost love, yet strike;
> Cast down, yet help afford;
> Sure I will do the like.
>
> I will complain, yet praise;
> I will bewail, approve:
> And all my sowre-sweet dayes
> I will lament, and love.
> (11.1–8)

This is Herbert at his most succinct. There are eleven clauses in eight lines, five lines having two clauses each in the six-syllable lines. The adversative clauses of the second stanza are typical and follow from those of the first, as does the use of the adversative conjunction *yet* in the first line. In the second line, the conjunction is omitted and this, too, is characteristic of Herbert's style. In the final line, the apparently opposing verbs are linked by *and*. The use of the co-ordinating conjunction has the effect of uniting rather than contrasting the two clauses. The to and fro movement of the preceding lines ceases as the object of the first verb in the line *lament* shifts suddenly from God to the speaker, who laments his own conduct but worships his Maker. The verbs become part of a single movement towards God, although directed at different objects. *Lament* and *love* do not represent contrary attitudes as do the verbs in the preceding lines and the reconciliation implied here is reinforced by alliteration.

The very short clauses of 'Bitter-sweet' are partly dictated by the verse form and, naturally, not all Herbert's clauses or clause complexes are so short. Frequently a clause complex, consisting of three or four clauses, will take up an entire stanza or most of it. An example where each stanza is one clause complex is the first half of 'The H. Communion'. The first stanza shows how Herbert builds up his sentence through the six lines:

> Not in rich furniture, or fine aray,
>   Nor in a wedge of gold,
>   Thou, who for me wast sold,
>   To me dost now thy self convey;
> For so thou should'st without me still have been,
>   Leaving within me sinne.
> (11.1–6)

In the first stanza the initial clause takes up four lines, with an interposed non-restrictive relative clause in the third line. The main verb is delayed until the end of the fourth line. The third clause is linked by a co-ordinating conjunction *for* with an *-ing* clause rounding off the stanza in the final line. Co-ordination and *-ing* clauses form the entire means of linking in this four-stanza poem, apart from a final clause joined with the subordinating conjunction *While*:

> While those to spirits refin'd, at doore attend
> Dispatches from their friend.
> (11.23–4)

All the clauses are right-branching, except in the first stanza, which has the interposed relative clause. That apart, the subordinate clauses follow their main clauses. This is Herbert's usual method, although there are occasional interposed clauses and he sometimes places a subordinate before a main clause. One parenthetical clause, marked by brackets, comes at the beginning of 'S. Marie Magdalene':

> When blessed Marie wip'd her Saviours feet,
> (Whose precepts she had trampled on before) ...
> (11.1–2)[4]

The reminder of Magdalene's past life is neatly inserted and linked to the story of washing Christ's feet by the word *trampled*. Extrapolated clauses also occur, as in the first line of 'Affliction' (IV), in which a description of the complement of the main clause is preposed:

> Broken in pieces all asunder,
> Lord, hunt me not.
> (11.1–2)

The clause which semantically postmodifies *me* becomes thematically marked by its initial placing in the sentence and thus immediately focuses the reader's attention on the topic of the sentence and of the poem, the tortured condition of the sinner.[5] These deviations from the norm are rare, however. Clause elements are sometimes inverted. Herbert often places adverbial groups in front of the complement or initially in the clause. But the position of adverbials is somewhat freer in any case. Herbert usually follows the normal S V C order of the clause elements in English.

He also uses appositive structures. Many of these consist of nominal groups, which derive from 'the catalogue of delights' in pastoral poetry, and from the *blazons* of the love-lyric'. They may be found in the sonnets of Sidney and Spenser amongst others.[6] The most obvious of Herbert's examples are 'Prayer' (I) and the first stanza of 'Sunday', but several poems have shorter appositive lists. One which has a series of negated groups is 'The Quidditie':

> ... a verse is not a crown,
> No point of honour, or gay suit,
> No hawk, or banquet, or renown,
> Nor a good sword, nor yet a lute.
> (11.1–4)

The second stanza contains appositive-type clauses in which the frame is the same for each. The second two are elliptical and contain only the lexical verb besides the conjunction:

> It cannot vault, or dance, or play;
> It never was in *France* or *Spain*;
> Nor can it entertain the day
> With my great stable or demain.
> (11.5–8)

'To all Angels and Saints' mixes appositive clauses and nominal groups that are longer than usual:

> Thou art the holy mine, whence came the gold,
> The great restorative for all decay
>   In young and old:
> Thou art the cabinet where the jewell lay.
> (11.11–14)

It is partly because his sentences generally follow normal word and clause order that Herbert's verse conveys the sense of a speaking voice. Like Donne's, his poems frequently begin with a direct address, often to the deity:

> Lord, how couldst thou so much appease
> Thy wrath for sinne ...
> ('Faith' 11.1–2)

or:

> My God, I heard this day,
> That none doth build a stately habitation,
> But he that means to dwell therein.
> ('Man' 11.1–3)

Questions and exclamations are other common means of starting a poem and these too give the illusion of speech. Herbert, even more than Donne, sustains the simulation of speech through the whole poem. Frequently he uses ordinary speech-fillers, such as *well* and *sure*:

> Sure thou wilt joy, by gaining me;
> ('The Starre' 1.29)

> Well, I will change the service.
> ('Affliction' (I) 1.63)

Another speech connector used is *besides*:

> Besides, things sort not to my will.
> ('The Crosse' 1.19)

Herbert's rhythms, too, reinforce the sense of speech. Short-lined stanzas and those with alternating longer and shorter lines vary the movement in a way that seems to mirror speech rhythms. We see this in 'The Discharge':

> Busie enquiring heart, what wouldst thou know?
> Why dost thou prie,
> And turn, and leer, and with a licorous eye
> Look high and low;
> And in thy lookings stretch and grow?
> (11.1–5)

The metre is further counterpointed by the running on of some lines. This can result in longer or shorter rhythmic speech units. It is this seeming unpredictableness that makes for the illusion of speech. The breaking of longer lines into short clauses, as in the third line above, also varies rhythm and speed. In these poems, especially, rhyme is important for marking the line endings for the reader's ear. It thereby provides a frame within which the various lengths and rhythms of clause are set. Perhaps because there is less stress shift, Herbert's verse reads more smoothly than that of Donne. Nevertheless, in the longer-lined stanzas and those which contain more lines, he often has mid-line breaks, sometimes suddenly, as in 'The Crosse':

> What is this strange and uncouth thing?
> To make me sigh, and seek, and faint, and die,
> Untill I had some place, where I might sing,
>   And serve thee; and not onely I,
> But all my wealth and familie might combine
> To set thy honour up, as our designe.
>   (11.1–6)

Here the first three and a half lines gather momentum, starting with the series of co-ordinated verbs and continuing with short but linked clauses, all held together by the same subject, until the movement stops at the semi-colon after *thee*. Then a counter thought: 'and not onely I', seems to interrupt the flow, bursting in upon it much in the fashion of speech. Thereafter the focus changes from the *me/I* of the first lines to other subjects. Similar, and even more startling reversals, often come at the ends of poems, as the well-known reversals in 'Affliction' (I) and 'The Collar'. Even in 'The Church-Porch', essentially a didactic poem and very measured in its pace, there is a sudden speech-like outburst:

> O be drest;
> Stay not for th'other pin.
>   (11.410–11)

Herbert's language is generally colloquial and this, too, adds to the sense of speech. Verbs such as *prie* and the phrasal verbs *set up* and *seek out*; the adjective *stout* in the sense of 'strong' and the expression *though I am clean forgot*, meaning 'though I wholly forget myself', all contribute to the informality. More colloquial words are found elsewhere, such as the nouns *brunt* and *brags* and the verbs *gad*; *snudge* and *jogs*.

Herbert makes much less use of pro-forms than Donne and much less obtrusively. Just occasionally we find an instance similar to Donne's:

> All things are busie; onely I
> Neither bring hony with the bees,
> Nor flowres to make *that*, nor the husbandrie
> To water *these*.
> ('Employment' (I) 11.17–20) [my italics]

A necessary corollary of the pro-forms is ellipsis. An example with an ellipted verb is:

> Love is that liquour sweet and most divine,
> Which my God feels as bloud; but I, as wine;
> ('The Agonie' 11.17–18)

and with the first pronoun in the second line omitted:

> Be not Almightie, let me say,
> Against, but for me.
> ('The Search' 11.51–2)

Again, the parenthetical *let me say* is conversational. The last line of the following from 'Good Friday' has the pro-form *all* and ellipts most of the clause:

> Shall I thy woes
> Number according to thy foes?
> Or, since one starre show'd thy first breath,
> Shall all thy death?
> (11.5–8)

More often Herbert is aphoristic. This is especially noticeable in 'The Church-Porch', which contains frequent apothegms, such as

'Kneeling ne're spoil'd silk stocking' (1.407). Herbert's hallmarks are terseness and economy of expression.

Verbal groups are often short, many verbs being in the imperative mood. This comes of Herbert's didacticism. Many poems, too, are framed as prayers or petitions, which require imperatives. Edgecombe has noted Herbert's indebtedness to the form of syntax found in the Collects.[7] Many of the Collects have the syntactical form: 1) a vocative; 2) an amplifying relative or adjectival clause; 3) one or more imperatives; 4) a clause of result, sometimes including a relative or -*ing* clause after the subject; 5) a final prepositional phrase, usually 'Through Jesus Christ our Lord'. Only the vocative and imperative are always included and the order can vary. A typical example is the Collect for the Sixth Sunday after Trinity:

> O God, who has prepared for them that love thee such good things as pass man's understanding: Pour into our hearts such love toward thee, that we, loving thee above all things, may obtain thy promises, which exceed all that we can desire; through Jesus Christ our Lord.

Edgecombe says:

> So powerful is its influence that even if few of Herbert's poems show a complete reproduction of its pattern, some of its syntactic features recur in poem after poem.[8]

He cites 'Trinitie Sunday', in which the whole poem is cast in the pattern of a collect, as one of Herbert's fullest uses of this syntactical pattern. The final stanza of 'Deniall' is similar:

> O cheer and tune my heartlesse breast,
>   Deferre no time;
> That so thy favours granting my request,
>   They and my minde may chime,
>   And mend my ryme.
>   (11.26–30)

Here three imperatives make up the petition and these are followed by a lengthy adverbial clause of result, in which the 'disordered' rhyme of the previous stanzas is reconciled in the final line.

Apart from imperatives, many verbal groups consist of only the main verb. These are often more striking than Donne's, as the metaphorical use of *sting* in:

> ... poore bees, that work all day,
> Sting my delay.
> ('Praise' (I) 11.17–18)

Likewise, the nominal groups are often short, rarely premodified by more than one adjective and only occasionally postmodified by short prepositional adjuncts: *a wedge of gold* ('The H. Communion', 1.2); *this knot of man* ('Home', 1.61); *my inch of life* ('Complaining', 1.18) (note that none of these examples is premodified except by an article or possessive pronoun). A premodifying adjective occurs in *his poore cabinet of bone* ('Ungratefulnesse', 1.28) and, occasionally, a postmodifying prepositional group contains premodification: *The shells of fledge souls* ('Death', 1.11). Brief clauses are also postmodifiers: *the way that takes the town* ('Affliction' (I), 1.38); *a man that looks on glasse* ('The Elixir', 1.9); and with premodification of the head noun: *the famous stone/ That turneth all to gold* ('The Elixir', 11.21–2). The brevity of the clause elements, especially subjects and complements, partly accounts for short clauses and Herbert's terse, although seldom abrupt, style.

Herbert's poems give the impression of being tight-knit texts, in spite of the fact that many lack strong inter-sentence cohesion on the lexical and grammatical levels. There is frequent omission of overt connectives. This poses a problem: if the lexico-grammatical connections are weak and the texture of the poems is loose in these ways, how can they be well-constructed texts? However, other factors enter into the texture of a unit of discourse besides lexis and the various grammatically cohesive devices, such as connectives and substitution.[9] One of these factors is register.[10] Herbert writes, almost wholly, in the register of the religious lyric. The reader, knowing this, makes the tacit assumption that however unlikely the statement in any given clause, it is certain to have some bearing on the customary subject matter. This, however, is not always a full answer to any intuitive connection the reader may need to make between clauses, as a brief example from 'Affliction' (I) will show:

> When I got health, thou took'st away my life,
>   And more; for my friends die:
> My mirth and edge was lost; a blunted knife
>   Was of more use then I.
>   (11.31–4)

The link between the second and third line is indicated by the colon, itself a cohesive device that is part of the structure of a text. However, it requires an imaginative step to make the semantic link. The second clause is consequent upon the first and the reader has to understand the implicit connection 'with the result that'. Herbert's poetry often takes for granted the reader's ability to make such connections. *Edge* is the lexical key to the next clause, which also lacks grammatical cohesion. The *blunted knife* picks up the sense of *edge*. At this point, the context has to be inferred by the reader. 'To be of use' must be understood in a religious sense, although the poem so far has dealt basically with the poet's disappointments in his secular career. Even when there is syntactical cohesion it can be misleading. The apparent grammatical connection of the subordinating conjunction at the beginning of the stanza can easily cause the reader to overlook the apparent semantic contradiction. How can a man 'get health' when his life is taken away? This must be understood in the context of the whole poem and, in particular, of the following stanza, in which the speaker's hopes of secular preferment, his 'life' or 'livelihood', were thwarted by his being consigned to academic studies. The reader must be alert to the connecting thread that sometimes runs counter to such grammatical connections as there are.

Another aspect of register that has already been touched on and which contributes to texture is the verse form and rhyme scheme that make up the frame for any one poem. Unlike Donne, who introduces extra syllables and stress shift, Herbert adheres rigidly to syllables, stress patterns and rhyme. The certainty of this frame helps to make up for the frequent lack of lexico-grammatical cohesion. 'Discipline' illustrates this clearly. The versification is strictly followed through every one of the eight short stanzas. Furthermore, the syntax combines with the metre to produce a tight-knit structure. Short, asyndetic clauses occur throughout, although there is a considerable amount of cohesive lexical repetition. Herbert repeats the verb in the first two clauses but the same syntactical frame occurs in all three: V^{imp} C, with an initial vocative introducing the final clause:

> Throw away thy rod,
> Throw away thy wrath:
> O my God,
> Take the gentle path.
> (11.1–4)

The fifth stanza is similarly constructed:

> Love is swift of foot;
> Love's a man of warre,
> And can shoot,
> And can hit from farre.
> (11.21–4)

The two pairs of lines here have the same frames. The first two lines have subject, verb and complement, and the second two a conjunction and verbal group. The only differences in pattern are the noun for adjective in the second line, and the addition of a brief adverbial adjunct in the last line. Moreover, the final stanza partially repeats the first:

> Throw away thy rod;
> Though man frailties hath,
> Thou art God:
> Throw away thy wrath.
> (11.29–32)

This closes the circular pattern and completes the tightness of the whole structure.

Another way in which Herbert creates texture in his poems is by his use of metaphor. Walter Nash speaks of 'the organizing metaphor':

> Patterns of multivalence, associative shifts in which meanings expand, splinter, and re-form like the coloured fragments in a kaleidoscope, often occur because the writer's mind is powerfully seized by some explanatory image or analogue.[11]

A poem that is organized through a metaphor drawn from music is 'Easter'. In the first stanza the music metaphor is marginal. There is only one reference: to the act of singing in the imperative clause, *Sing his praise*. This sounds literal but must be metaphorical since it is the speaker's 'heart' that is being thus admonished. The second stanza begins with a conventional metaphor of the same kind, a command addressed to his lute, before it moves into a more highly-wrought conceit:

> Awake, my lute, and struggle for thy part
> With all thy art.
> The crosse taught all wood to resound his name,
> Who bore the same.
> His stretched sinews taught all strings, what key
> Is best to celebrate this most high day.
> (11.7–12)

The celebration of the festival with music is interwoven with the physical suffering of Christ.[12] The language is metaphorical but also concrete and apt. The word *key*, in particular, has a precision in musical terms that tightens the whole image. The final stanza elaborates on the act of making music. This is expressed more literally again, except that the actors are the 'heart' (picked up from the first stanza) and 'lute' (from the second). Through reasoning worthy of Donne, Herbert draws on the technicalities of music as it was practised at the time to include the Holy Spirit amongst the performers:

> Consort both heart and lute, and twist a song
> Pleasant and long:
> Or, since all musick is but three parts vied
> And multiplied,
> O let thy blessed Spirit bear a part,
> And make up our defects with his sweet art.
> (11.13–18)

Consort, a usage of the word as a verb now obsolete, is a musical term referring to the harmonious unison of 'instruments'. The third and fourth lines are puzzling but seem to mean that harmony must be made up of three or more parts. The mention of 'three parts', the third being taken by the Holy Spirit, hints at the Trinity. The musical metaphor, which unifies this poem, is here a vehicle for forwarding what for Herbert was the literal meaning of Easter, the reuniting of Christ in the Trinity.

Another short poem that is organized through a metaphor is 'Life', and again Herbert shifts between metaphorical and literal modes. The first stanza reads:

> I made a posie, while the day ran by:
> Here will I smell my remnant out, and tie
> My life within this band.
> But Time did becken to the flowers, and they
> By noon most cunningly did steal away,
> And wither'd in my hand.
>
> (11.1–6)

It is possible to take the whole poem as an emblem of 'Life'. The *posie* is an emblem in a very literal sense. The first meaning of *posy*, which derives from *poesy*, is a motto or line of verse and hence an emblem. The use of the word to denote a small bunch of flowers or nosegay developed later.[13] Here Herbert evokes both senses in a sort of word play. The making of the flower 'posy' is both literal and figurative – organizing one's life: 'tie/ My life within this band'. The first line of the second stanza indicates the duality of signification: 'My hand was next to them, (literal) and then my heart (metaphorical)'. The rest of the poem hangs on this initial establishment of the metaphor and must be read on two levels. The first three lines of the final stanza are strictly literal, although the application of the comments on the flowers to man is implicit:

> Farewell deare flowers, sweetly your time ye spent,
> Fit, while ye liv'd, for smell or ornament,
> And after death for cures.
>
> (11.13–15)

The final statement is made from the speaker's viewpoint but explicitly relates the human condition to that of the flowers:

> I follow straight without complaints or grief,
> Since if my sent [scent] be good, I care not if
> It be as short as yours.
>
> (11.16–18)

Many poems have some kind of metaphorical structure, sometimes overt, sometimes implicit. The reader must understand the different layers of meaning which give the poems their cohesion and texture.

In various ways, therefore, Herbert's poems are coherent texts, having a closely woven texture, even in those poems which are lacking in certain lexico-grammatical links that might be expected. Of course, not all of his poems are loose in this way. Many of the near-narrative poems, such as 'Redemption', and others, such as 'The Pulley', are lexically and grammatically cohesive, and have also the textural qualities just discussed.

Some of Herbert's figurative language and imagery has already been looked at. Although he says, 'Riddle who list for me' ('Jordan' (I), 1.12), he follows the Elizabethan tradition of riddling, as in the use of emblems and emblematic titles. This kind of writing characterizes Herbert's verse. The emblems are usually well-known Christian symbols rather than the conventional emblems of the sixteenth-century emblem books. Some of these have been examined. The idea of life on earth as a pilgrimage, which runs through Francis Quarles's series of emblems illustrating the trials of *Anima*, is dramatized in the poem 'The Pilgrimage'. This brief allegory prefigures Vaughan's 'Regeneration', although some of the landmarks on the speaker's journey, 'The gloomy cave of Desperation' (1.4); 'Cares cops' (1.11); and the 'lake of brackish waters' (1.23) are more akin to Bunyan's *Pilgrim's Progress* (1678). An example of an emblematic poem in the Jesuitical tradition that grew up in the seventeenth century is 'Love unknown'. The central symbol or emblem is the *heart*, which is 'dipt and dy'd/ And washt and wrung' and finally flung into a 'boyling caldron' to make it clean and tender. This is a somewhat unusual type of emblem for Herbert and more in the spirit of Crashaw.

Repetition in various forms is a favourite rhetorical device.[14] It frequently takes the form of *ploce*, the repetition of words at frequent intervals. An instance of verbal play and repetition mentioned earlier was the variation on *rest* and *restlessnesse* (*polyptoton*) in 'The Pulley' (pp.52–3). A similar example occurs in 'Deniall':

> O that thou shouldst give dust a tongue
> To crie to thee,
> And then not heare it crying!
> (11.16–18)

The reiteration of *crying* both emphasizes the word itself and, coupled with the negative, adds force to the tragic pitifulness. A repetition, involving a change of the medial vowel, which slightly alters the sense of the word, comes in 'The Dawning':

> Do not by hanging down break from the hand,
> Which as it riseth, raiseth thee.
> (11.11–12)

The visual effect comes from the emblem-like picture of the hand reaching down to draw the man upwards. In 'Repentance', Herbert uses chiastic repetition in which the same words are repeated in reverse order (*antimetabole*):

> Lord, I confess my sinne is great;
> Great is my sinne.
> (11.1–2)

The repetition focuses attention on the sinner's need for repentance. *Great* becomes thematic in the second repetition, thus emphasizing the enormity of the *sinne*. A similar chiasmus occurs in 'Love' (I):

> Wit fancies beautie, beautie raiseth wit.
> (1.9)

The subject and complement of the second clause are the same as the first with a change of verb.

Immediate repetition of a word (*epizeuxis*) is frequent. In 'Affliction' (IV) it is used as the resumptive device *anadiplosis*: the use of the word at the end of a clause to start the next. Herbert appears to use this type of repetition as a means of pushing the poem forward:

> Lord, hunt me not,
> A thing forgot,
> Once a poore creature, now a wonder,
> A wonder tortur'd in the space
> Betwixt this world and that of grace.
> (11.2–6)

Alliteration is comparatively rare in Herbert's poetry and when it does occur is decorative rather than affective. One example, which is more integrated into the meaning than most, comes near the beginning of 'The Collar':

> My lines and life are free; free as the rode,
> Loose as the winde, as large as store.
> (11.4–5)

An initial /l/ is repeated four times in the two lines. The first two instances impart a fluid, joyful quality, which, coupled with the meaning of *free*, contrasts with the bondage which the speaker mentions immediately after. *Free* is emphasized by *anadiplosis* and the sense of freedom is further developed in the two following complement phrases, which each repeat the /l/ sound of *lines and life*. In this way the sense of the opening lines is underlined by alliteration.

Another device that Herbert uses sparingly is punning. It is not clear if the occasional pun is intentional or fortuitous. There appears to be a pun on the words *bindes* and *bound* in the second stanza of 'Mortification':

> When boyes go first to bed,
> They step into their voluntarie graves,
>   Sleep bindes them fast; onely their breath
>   Makes them not dead:
> Successive nights, like rolling waves,
> Convey them quickly, who are bound for death.
> (11.7–12)

If alliteration and punning occur only sporadically in Herbert's verse, personification is used freely with deliberate intent. At times it appears in its traditional form, an abstract quality being personified, as the emblematic figure in 'Humilitie':

> Humilitie, who held the plume, at this
> Did weep so fast, that the tears trickling down
> Spoil'd all the train.
> (11.25–7)

More arresting, however, are Herbert's dramatic uses of personification. An example which would be unintelligible without the title of the poem: 'Conscience', takes the form of a monologue, the poet being the speaker:

> Peace pratler, do not lowre:
> Not a fair look, but thou dost call it foul:
> Not a sweet dish, but thou dost call it sowre;
> (11.1–3)

and so on through four stanzas, Here again, ellipsis gives the sense of a speaking voice. In the last two lines quoted, there is alliteration: *fair* and *foul*, and *sweet* and *sowre*.

'Time' is another poem that is presented in this dramatic way:

> Meeting with Time, Slack thing, said I,
> Thy sithe is dull; whet it for shame.
> No marvell Sir, he did replie,
> If it at length deserve some blame:
> But where one man would have me grinde it,
> Twentie for one too sharp do finde it.
> (11.1–6)

The speaker then harangues *Time* on this statement until finally *Time* breaks out in a disgusted aside:

> This man deludes:
> What do I here before his doore?
> He doth not crave lesse time, but more.
> (11.29–30)

One of the most effective of Herbert's dramatic presentations of personification is 'The Quip':

> The merrie world did on a day
> With his train-bands and mates agree
> To meet together, where I lay,
> And all in sport to geere at me.
> (11.1–4)

In subsequent stanzas *Beautie*; *Money*; *Glorie* and *Wit* and

Conversation all mock the speaker. Some of the brief speeches of these personifications are particularly striking for their jeering tone. When the speaker refuses to pluck a rose, *Beautie* cries:

> Tell me, I pray, Whose hands are those?
> (1.7)

and *Money*, jingles his gold with:

> What tune is this, poore man? said he:
> I heard in Musick you had skill.
> (11.9–10)

The best-known and the most skilful of these dramatic personifications comes in the poem called 'Love' (III). *Love* invites the speaker of the poem to a meal, presumably the Communion. Here is genuine dialogue which carries the poem through to its conclusion. In the middle stanza, after *Love* has asked if anything is lacking, the poem continues:

> A guest, I answer'd, worthy to be here:
> Love said, You shall be he.
> I the unkinde, ungratefull? Ah my deare,
> I cannot look on thee.
> Love took my hand, and smiling did reply,
> Who made the eyes but I?
> (11.7–12)

The climax of the poem is reached at the end of the fourth line here, and subsequently the arguments are countered until the speaker acquiesces with:

> So I did sit and eat.
> (1.18)

There may be another pun in the final line of the stanza quoted on the two words *eyes* and *I*. This poem can also be read as a narrative-type emblem in the style of Quarles's depictions of *Amor* and *Anima*.

The most constant feature of Herbert's figurative language is metaphor, as we saw when exploring texture. Herbert speaks belittlingly of metaphor in 'Jordan' (II). He says that in his early poems:

> My thoughts began to burnish, sprout, and swell,
> Curling with metaphors a plain intention,
> Decking the sense, as if it were to sell.
> (11.4–6)

Nevertheless, he did not drop the metaphorical mode as he himself recognized. In 'The Forerunners', which appears to have been written towards the end of his life, he says:

> Farewell sweet phrases, lovely metaphors.
> But will ye leave me thus? when ye before
> Of stews and brothels onely knew the doores,
> Then did I wash you with my tears, and more,
>   Brought you to Church well drest and clad:
> My God must have my best, ev'n all I had.
> (11.13–18)

Now, after he has converted the secular use of figurative language to religious purposes, inspiration is failing him. Throughout the *The Temple* every type of metaphor has been used. Besides the intricate and extended metaphors examined earlier, others are short and so integrated into the language that they are often called 'dead', as in 'Deniall':

> Then was my heart broken, as was my verse.
> (1.3)

Broken hearts are a part of everyday language although they cannot be broken in a literal sense. Whether verse can be said to be literally 'broken' is more difficult to determine. Other metaphors, as with so much of his language, are drawn from everyday domestic living. It has been said that:

> To convince us that his interest in the circumstances of his daily life was not entirely conventional or casual a writer's images from this source would have to be at once recurrent, studied, peculiar to him, and characterized by a certain amount of imaginative excitement.[15]

Herbert's everyday imagery frequently has just such 'imaginative excitement'. It is certainly 'recurrent' and 'studied' and 'peculiar to him' in its conception, even when it is related to conventional Christian images or emblems that would have been familiar to his readers from other sources. One example of a very striking homely image that is rarely commented on is in 'The Church-Porch':

> God gave thy soul brave wings; put not those feathers
> Into a bed, to sleep out all ill weathers.
> (11.83–4)

The image of the feather bed is Herbert's own. Other domestic images are less surprising but just as vital. A brief example of a simile is the following from 'Church-lock and key':

> ... as cold hands are angrie with the fire,
>   And mend it still;
> So I do lay the want of my desire,
> Not on my sinnes, or coldnesse, but thy will.
> (11.5–8)

This is ambiguous. The *cold hands* could be literal or they could be *metonymic*, in this instance a part of the body denoting the whole person. In the first case, the word *angrie* has the meaning of 'red, raw or chafed'. In the second, it is a type of transferred epithet, *angrie* being the emotion felt by the person to whom the hands belong. In context, the second reading seems more likely. In either case the image is highly visual and the language compressed. A metaphor from domestic life, which is immediately followed by a simile taken from gardening, comes in 'Affliction' (IV):

> My thoughts are all a case of knives,
>   Wounding my heart
>   With scatter'd smart,
> As watring pots give flowers their lives.
> (11.7–10)

Herbert's rhythmic control is so smooth that the unexpectedness of the meaning expressed in the simile is easily overlooked. The wounds are strangely life-giving. We might have expected a comparison drawn from the crucifixion at this point but instead Herbert uses another domestic picture.

Compared with the intellectualism of Donne's figurative language, Herbert achieves an intellectual approach to his subject matter through concrete and domestic imagery that frequently utilizes conventional symbols already known to his readers. It is the way in which he succeeds in stamping his own highly personal imprint on this integration of imagery from traditional Christian sources with glimpses of domestic and essentially everyday activity that gives his poetry its peculiar force. Through language, rich in its possibilities of interpretation, Herbert explicates the abstract mysteries of Christianity and the Christian experience.

4 Richard Crashaw (1612–1649)

'strong Extasy'
('Musicks Duell')

Many of Crashaw's major poems are versions of Latin or Italian originals. Some, such as *Sospetto d'Herode* from Marino's Italian,[1] are fairly close translations, at least in substance, while others, such as the medieval hymns, are paraphrases and follow the originals loosely. All are English poems in their own right and this book does not examine the language of translation. Crashaw's first publication, in 1634, when he was only twenty-two years old, was a collection of Latin epigrams. These are translations from English into Latin based on the biblical readings set in the *Book of Common Prayer*.[2] They are, however, the result of exercises in the art of translating and composing Latin epigrams performed when he was a schoolboy at the Charterhouse and a student at Pembroke College, Cambridge. Translation affected Crashaw's English style, especially his use of figurative language and, to some extent, his syntax. Early training in the epigrammatic tradition was the strongest influence on his language. His vocabulary, however, seems to have been comparatively little affected.

It is vocabulary that markedly differentiates Crashaw's verse from that of Herbert. Herbert's 'household stuffe' is that of the country house and park or garden. Crashaw uses the same phrase but, as he implies, his is the furniture of heaven:

Come, ye soft ministers of sweet sad mirth,
Bring All your houshold stuffe of Heaun on earth.
('To the Name of Iesus' 11.62–3)

Although the bulk of Crashaw's most important poems, and the ones we shall concentrate on here, has, like Herbert's, religion for its theme, the diction of the poems differs in many ways. The diction affects his imagery and the entire reach of his verse, even though, in other respects, he relies on many of the devices used by both Donne and Herbert.

Much of Crashaw's vocabulary derives, like that of Donne and Herbert, from native Old English stock and is frequently monosyllabic, although he uses considerably more words of Latin and Romance origin. In one sense, his vocabulary is concrete but it is used in an emblematic rather than in a literally concrete manner. Ruth Wallerstein, speaking of Crashaw's use of adjectives, says:

> "Soft" becomes in Crashaw's poetry a pure adjective of sentiment and "white" passes through a sense of radiance or brilliance – perhaps with some recollection of "candidus" – to become a pure symbol of "exaltation".[3]

What is true of adjectives applies also to the rest of his vocabulary. It is partly Crashaw's idiosyncratic use of symbols and the emblem tradition that has led critics to call his language 'baroque'. It corresponds in words to the visual impressions of the architecture and decoration of the baroque churches in southern and central Europe.

Heart and *breast* are two of the most frequently used nouns, along with other parts of the human body, such as *eyes*; *hands*; *feet* and also *hair*, as the subject matter demands. The last three, for instance, are prominent in references to Mary Magdalene, who is remembered for washing Christ's feet with her tears and drying them with her hair. *Tears*, both in the singular and plural, is another much used noun, as is *kiss*. Many critics have noted how often Crashaw rhymes *breast* with *nest*. *Dove* is also a frequent word, which, besides collocating with *nest* and conveniently rhyming with *love*, has biblical associations. A passage which includes several of these words comes in 'The Weeper':

> O cheeks! Bedds of chast loues,
> By your own showres seasonably dash't
> Eyes! nests of milky doues.
> (11.85–7)

Such verbal associations show the eroticism of Crashaw's imaginative insight. Not all nouns denote the gentler side of the Christian story: many, perhaps more, refer to Christ's suffering. The almost pastoral lyricism of 'A Hymne on the Nativity' is very close in manner to Milton's 'On the Morning of Christs Nativity' (1629). Generally, however, Crashaw dwells on the agony of Christ's death and the martyrdom of his disciples. Words such as *blood*; *wounds*; *spear*; *cross*; *flame* and *fire* are found time and again.

Crashaw's nouns are usually lexically fuller than his verbs, although at times he uses both in complementary pairs: *blood* and *bleed*; *tears* and *weep*. One line from 'The Mother of Sorrowes' contains all four with the related nouns and verbs switched:

> Her eyes bleed TEARES, his wounds weep BLOOD.
> (1.20)

The verbs, however, can be forceful in context even if not strictly dynamic or semantically action verbs in themselves. *Write* for example, in the clause: 'His Nailes write swords in her', gains vitality from its unexpected subject and complement: *Nailes* and *swords*. *Turn*, which is a resulting copular verb, continues the metaphor:

> Her SWORDS, still growing with his pain,
> Turn SPEARES, & straight come home again.
> (11.29–30)

The same access of energy applies to *growing* and *come*. In the latter case, the preceding adverb *straight* gives the verb particular force. The verbs in this stanza from 'The Mother of Sorrowes' mark the energetic thrust of a swift moving debate, reflecting the silent 'discourse' that takes place between the emotions of Christ and his mother. An example of another verb that gains strength from its context is *shrink* in *Sospetto d'Herode*:

That the Great Angell-blinding light should shrinke
His blaze, to shine in a poore Shepheards eye.
(11.169–70)

Occasionally verbs are themselves striking, as *'vncase'* in *'vncase/ A soul'* ('Hymn to Sainte Teresa', 1.72); *stagger* in 'When starres themselues shall *stagger'* (*Dies Irae*, 1.23); *dazle* in *'dazle* my darke Mysteries' (*Sospetto d'Herode*, 1.232) and *broach* in 'new *broach* the Mountaines' (l.112). This again, because of its metaphorical use, can hardly be understood out of context:

Hee [Satan] saw a vernall smile, sweetly disfigure
Winters sad face, and through the flowry lands
Of fair *Engaddi* hony-sweating Fountaines
With *Manna*, Milk, and Balm, new broach
the Mountaines.
(*Sospetto d'Herode*, 11.109–12)

Disfigure in the first line sounds strange in this context but must be understood in its etymological meaning of 'reversing or negating the shape'. Another effective use of verbs in a similar context occurs in 'A Hymne of the Nativity':

The North forgott his feirce Intent;
And left perfumes, in stead of scarres.
By those sweet eyes' persuasiue powrs,
Where he mean't frost, he scatter'd flowrs.
(11.26–9)

The attitudinal stative verb *meant* becomes dynamic in context. The impact of the verbs is one of the chief differences that distinguishes Crashaw's translations from their originals.[4]

Crashaw uses adjectives more obviously than either Herbert or Donne. His emblematic or subliminal use of sense adjectives has been mentioned. Many of the adjectives are sensuous and cloying to modern taste. *Sweet*; *soft* and *milky* are frequent. Similar is *delicious*, which is almost always used in combination with a noun denoting some form of suffering. So we find '*delicious* wounds' ('Hymn to Sainte Teresa'); '*delicious* fire' ('Song') and '*delicious* deaths' ('On a Prayer booke'). Crashaw exults in pain and suffering and this is also in line with the baroque nature of his verse. Occasionally there are compound adjectives and these, too, can stress the sensuous aspect of pain, as in *'sweetly-killing dart'* ('Hymn to Sainte Teresa'). Some appear to contradict the meaning of the noun which they premodify, as in *'still-suruiuing funerall'* ('Hymn to Sainte Teresa'); others are simply striking for their aptness and compression, as in *deep-digg'd side* ('Vpon the Bleeding Crucifix'). When they involve a paradox or puzzle the context is needed for solving the riddle. Even then the meaning is not always clear. In 'A Hymne of the Nativity' the context does little to elucidate the meaning of *well-stoln*:

> To all our world of well-stoln joy
> He slept; and dream't of no such thing.
> (11.5–6)

Neither does the context in 'A Hymn to Sainte Teresa' explain how the *funerall* can be *still-suruiuing*:

> Into loue's armes thou shalt let fall
> A still-suruiuing funerall.
> (11.77–8)

The meaning is partly made clear by the *oxymoron* and apparent contradictions in the lines that come a little later:

> ... a DEATH, in which who dyes
> Loues his death, and dyes again.
> And would for euer so be slain.
> And liues, & dyes; and knowes not why
> To liue, But that he thus may neuer leaue to DY.
> (11.100–04)

This is the 'death more mysticall & high', which Teresa must undergo; the 'milder MARTYRDOM' to which she is called. It is the paradox of the Christian religion, based on Christ's saying in Matthew X.39. 'He that findeth his life shall lose it: and he that loseth his life for my sake shall find it'. These paradoxes are all examples of Crashaw's 'knotty riddles', which are less easy to unravel than either Herbert's or Donne's.

Colour adjectives occur frequently in Crashaw's verse. These are often variations of the colour red. The associations with blood are obvious. Rarely does Crashaw simply refer to blood with a single premodifying colour adjective. He prefers circumlocution, such as *the purple wardrobe in thy side* ('Vpon the Body of Our Blessed Lord') or *this red sea of thy blood* ('Vpon the Bleeding Crucifix'). The noun *blush* in *blush of Thine Own blood* ('The Name of Iesus') obviates the need for a colour adjective with the noun. In other places the blood shed at the crucifixion is implicit rather than stated. An example occurs in *Vexilla Regis*, in which the cross is apostrophized as 'Larg throne of loue!' The verse continues:

> Royally spred
> With purple of too Rich a red.
> (11.25–6)

The two colour words are both grammatically nouns, but here there is little point in differentiating between nouns and adjectives. Often the word *blood* is left unmodified and itself conjures up the image of red. Closely connected to the red of blood is the colour of wine, especially sacramental communion wine. We find '*purpling* vine' ('The Weeper') and '*rosy* nectar' ('An Apologie'). *Rosy* is one of Crashaw's most used words in this group and is applied variously: '*rosy* fingers' ('The Flaming Heart'); '*Rosy* hand' ('The Flaming Heart'); '*rosy* princesse' ('On the Assumption') and '*Rosy* Nest' ('To the Name of Iesus'). The poem usually known as 'New Year's Day' also contains *rosy* amongst its many 'red' colour words. This is explained by its original title: 'An Himne for the Circumcision day of our Lord':

> Rise, thou best & brightest morning!
>   Rosy with a double Red;
> With thine own blush thy cheeks adorning
>   And the dear drops this day were shed.
>
> All the purple pride that laces,
>   The crimson curtains of thy bed,
> Guilds thee not with so sweet graces
>   Nor setts thee in so rich a red.
>   (11.1–8)

In these two stanzas, six words, seven if *Guilds* is included, are directly associated with red and, indirectly, with blood, although blood itself is not named. The *dear drops* are the blood of the circumcision, the second meaning implied in the description of the dawn as being a *double Red*. The phrase *Rich a red* occurred earlier. Crashaw was probably drawn to this combination because of the alliteration. The voluptuousness of the colour is also strengthened by the adjective *rich*. The verb *Guilds* recalls Shakespeare's use in *Macbeth*:

> *Lady Macbeth*: If he do bleed
> I'll gild the faces of the grooms withal.
> (II. ii.54–5)

Another much used 'red' word is *ruby*, as in 'the *Ruby* portalls of the East' (*Sospetto d'Herode*) and '*Ruby* windowes' ('To the Name of Iesus'). *Red* itself is found less often as an adjectival premodifier than might be expected, although there are instances: '*Red* cheeks' ('The Flaming Heart'). More often it occurs predicatively, as in the previous quotation, or as a noun, as in *Dies Irae*:

> The conscious colors of my sin
> Are red without & pale within.
> (11.43–4)

Here, *pale*, with its implication of 'white', suggests the inner death that sin works on the individual. The word *white* itself might be expected to appear more than it does. It occurs in *Charitas Nimia*:

> Why should the white
> Lamb's bosom write
> The purple name
> Of my sin's shame?
> (11.57–60)

Sins are here associated with *purple*. *White* is used of the redeeming power of the *Lamb*: Christ. Crashaw, however, concentrates less on the redemptive and pure aspect of the 'sacrificial' Christ and more on his agony at the crucifixion. Often 'white' is implicit in words such as *snow*; *breasts*; *milk* and, on occasion, *lily*. An effective juxtaposition of the two sacramental colours is found in sequential stanzas of 'A Hymne of the Nativity':

> I saw the curl'd drops, soft & slow,
>   Come houering o're the place's head;
> Offring their *whitest* sheets of *snow*
>   To furnish the fair INFANT'S bed
> Forbear, said I; be not too bold.
> Your fleece is *white* But t'is too cold.
>
> I saw the obsequious SERAPHIMS
>   Their *rosy* fleece of *fire* bestow.
> For well they now can spare their wings
>   Since HEAVN itself lyes here below.
> Well done, said I: but are you sure
> Your down so warm, will passe for pure?[5]
>   (11.51–64) [my italics]

The opposition of the *whitest sheets of snow* and the *rosy fleece of fire*, both offered as a bed for the infant Christ, is neatly resolved by his choice of his mother's breast:

> Sweet choise, said we! no way but so
> Not to ly cold, yet sleep in snow.
>   (11.70–1)

As noted earlier, Crashaw uses a large number of words borrowed from Latin and Romance sources but these mingle naturally with words of native origin, as in 'To the Name of Iesus':

> In none but Thee
> And Thy *Nectareall Fragrancy*,
>   *Hourly* there meetes
> An *vniversall SYNOD* of All sweets.
>   (11.173–6) [my italics for Romance words]

Here five words of Romance (one Greek) origin come in three

lines. Two of them: *Nectareall* and *SYNOD* (Greek) are particularly striking. In the eleven lines preceding these there are sixteen Romance words. This mixture of the more basic and, at times, colloquial, native words with those that are elevated or literary, as in Donne and Herbert, is typical of the metaphysical poets: they sought unity in diversity, even in language itself. At times, either by accident or design, Crashaw shifts to words solely of native stock, so that a sudden effect of simplicity is achieved. Nowhere is this more obvious than in 'A Hymne of the Nativity':

>   Proud world, said I; *cease* your *contest*
>   And let the MIGHTY BABE alone.
>   The *Phaenix* builds the *Phaenix*' nest.
>   Love's *architecture* is his own.
>   The BABE whose birth *embraues* this morn,
>   Made his own bed e're he was born.
>   (11.45–50) [my italics]

The monosyllables of the final line stand out in stark contrast to the earlier vocabulary and the classical allusion to the phoenix.

Apart from vocabulary of religion and directly related topics, which is all pervasive, Crashaw draws words from other areas or registers. He has very occasional references to philosophy but these are so sporadic compared with Donne's as to amount more or less to ignoring the subject.

Like Herbert, Crashaw uses vocabulary from trade and commerce. *Charitas Nimia*, subtitled 'The Dear Bargain', which indicates the register, particularly makes use of it:

>   Loue is too kind, I see; & can
>   Make but a simple merchant man.
>   'Twas for such sorry merchandise
>   Bold Painters have putt out his Eyes.
>   (11.5–8)

Merchant man and *merchandise* carry on the metaphor, which is linked to Christ's love for man and, unexpectedly, to blind Cupid. The inference is that Christ's love is also blind in a worldly sense, since he pays over the odds for man's redemption. 'In the Glorious Epiphanie' affords another example:

> Maintaining t'wixt thy world & ours
> A commerce of contrary powres,
>   A mutuall trade
>   'Twixt sun & SHADE,
> By confederat BLACK & WHITE
> Borrowing day & lending night.
>   (11.214–19)

The first two lines prefigure Vaughan's 'busy commerce kept between/ God and his creatures ...', but the business image is extended in Crashaw's poem with the words *trade*; *confederat*; *Borrowing* and *lending*. The same type of vocabulary appears in 'A Hymn to Sainte Teresa':

> Sh'el to the Moores; And trade with them,
> For this vnualued Diadem.
> She'l offer them her dearest Breath,
> With CHRIST'S Name in't, in change for death.
> Sh'el bargain with them; & will giue
> Them GOD.
>   (11.47–52)

The child saint is depicted as a merchant, skilled in the business of trading.

Another register which yields much metaphorical vocabulary is warfare. Parallel examples can be found in both Donne and Herbert but in Crashaw's verse the subject is closely associated with the notion of the heavenly host. An emblematic example comes in 'A Hymn to Sainte Teresa':

> The fair'st & first-born sons of fire
> Blest SERAPHIM, shall leaue their quire
> And turn loue's souldiers, vpon THEE
> To exercise their archerie.
>   (11.93–6)

Another example of many that use this type of vocabulary is found in 'On a Prayer booke', a poem prefixed to a book of prayers that Crashaw gave to a 'young Gentlewoman':

> It is loue's great artillery
> Which here contracts it self, & comes to ly
> Close couch't in your white bosom: & from thence
> As from a snowy fortresse of defence.
>   (11.15–18)

The image is sustained through eight further lines.

The use of certain words over and over is a mark of Crashaw's style. Far from making his verse monotonous the accumulation of words, which are either emblematic or used metaphorically, gives the poetry its own coherence. The larger part of Crashaw's religious verse is lyric or 'rhapsodic', although most of the poems are longer than the lyrics of Donne and Herbert. Crashaw is essentially a lyric poet. The rhythms of his sentence structure often reflect the mood or subject matter of his verse.

In the 'rhapsodic' verse, Crashaw generally favours short clauses often linked by co-ordinate conjunctions or even avoiding connectives altogether. The clause length is partly dictated by the verse forms and metres, which have predominantly short lines, often irregular and varying from two to five feet within a single stanza in some poems. Crashaw's style tends to the exclamatory and this, too, leads to short clauses.

Many poems open with exclamations and apostrophes. In *Dies Irae* many of the early stanzas start with an exclamation: *O that fire!*; *O that trump!*; *Horror of nature, hell & Death!* The first stanza of 'The Weeper' has five appositive nominal groups, each an apostrophe to the eyes of Mary Magdalene:

>   Hail, sister springs!
>   Parents of syluer-footed rills!
>   Euer bubling things!
>   Thawing crystall! snowy hills,
>   Still spending, neuer spent!
>   (11.1–5)

Questions tend to appear in clusters, as in *Charitas Nimia*:

>   Lord, what is man? why should he coste thee
>   So dear? what has his ruin lost thee?
>   Lord what is man? that thou has ouerbought
>   So much a thing of nought?
>   (11.1–4)

Both exclamations and questions are sometimes cast in longer and more complex structures.

In the 'rhapsodic' verse, statements are often short. 'The Mother of Sorrowes' has relatively short clauses throughout, although these are often arranged to form quite lengthy clause complexes, as in the fourth stanza:

> She sees her son, her GOD,
> Bow with a load
> Of borrowd sins; And swimme
> In woes that were not made for Him.
> Ah hard command
> Of loue! Here must she stand
> Charg'd to look on, & with a stedfast ey
> See her life dy:
> Leauing her only so much Breath
> As serues to keep aliue her death.
> (11.31–40)

Although the individual clauses are short in this stanza, the sentences are relatively long. The whole stanza is built on two main clauses: *She sees her Son* and *Here must she stand*, with an exclamation separating the two halves. All the other clauses are dependent on one of these two statements. The last two lines present the most complex syntax. They are a participial clause, dependent on the second verb, *dy* of the preceding line. The complement, *so much Breath*, has a postmodifying correlative clause, which includes a dependent infinitive clause: *to keep aliue her death*. Both the structure and semantic paradox of these lines, which clinch the meaning of the whole stanza, are typical of Crashaw's epigrammatic style. Nine clauses in ten lines make up two sentences, with the additional verbless exclamatory clause. The somewhat jerky rhythmic effect of these short clauses, which are often broken in mid-line and run over the end of lines, conveys the impression of the woman's quick, shallow breathing, which is referred to in the final couplet. Crashaw usually writes more smoothly but his rhythmic effects are various. A basically simple clause structure is found throughout many of the poems, although the syntax can be more contorted, as in the following lines from 'The Weeper':

> Not in the euening's eyes
> When they Red with weeping are
> For the Sun that dyes,
> Sitts sorrow with a face so fair.
> (11.31–4)

Here the syntax is very compressed. *Not* is part of the adverbial phrase that it introduces and also relates to the deferred main clause in the last line. The easiest way to arrive at the sense is to read it thus: 'Sorrow does not sit with so fair a face even in the eyes of evening ...'. The imagery itself is compressed. Two pictures are superimposed: eyes red with weeping and the red sky at sunset. The emblematic image of the evening having eyes is so removed from the naturalistic that it is not easy to grasp, much less to visualize. It is truly metaphysical and a type of image that occurs more than once in Crashaw's verse.

Crashaw also wrote narrative verse. There are two main narrative poems: *Sospetto d'Herode* and the first part of 'A Hymn to Sainte Teresa'. The clauses in *Sospetto d'Herode* tend to be longer than in the other poems and, although the order in many clauses is the normal S V C, complex structures frequently occur. Verbs are often deferred until the end, or nearly the end, of a clause by interposed adverbials and frequent parenthetical phrases and clauses. The poem is written in eight-line stanzas and bears some resemblance to *Paradise Lost*, both in vocabulary and sentence structure.[6] A few lines give an idea of the syntax:

> Scarce to this Monster could the shady King,
> The horrid summe of his intentions tell;
> But shee (swift as the momentary wing
> Of lightning, or the words he spoke) left Hell.
> (11.369–72)

In the first clause the subject comes after two adjuncts and the auxiliary of the verbal group *could tell*. The lexical verb is placed after the complement in final position. In the second clause the verb precedes the complement but is again deferred until near the end by a lengthy parenthetical postmodifying adjectival phrase, which contains an embedded co-ordinate clause.

The first part of 'A Hymn to Sainte Teresa' has less complex syntax altogether. This may be because the subject is a child. The poem is written in rhyming couplets of octosyllabics and the lines are short. Even so the poem starts in a complex manner. After the initial address to 'Loue', the next sentence begins with a lengthy clause, running over eight whole and two half lines. The last two clauses briefly introduce the subject of the poem and initiate the shift to a more straightforward sentence structure:

> And see him take a priuate seat,
> Making his mansion in the mild
> And milky soul of a soft child.
> (ll.12–14)

The repeated /m/ and /s/ consonants have an onomatopoeic effect, conjuring up the idea of something gentle and soft. Sound, rhythm and syntax are virtually inseparable in Crashaw's writing. Every clause referring directly to Teresa and her actions or thoughts is expressed simply:

> Yet though she cannot tell you why,
> She can LOVE, & she can DY.
> (ll.23–4)

Here, three clauses make up the two lines and there is no inversion except for the introductory subordinate clause. Metaphorical expressions which relate to the child Teresa are also straightforward:

> Scarse has she Blood enough to make
> A guilty sword blush for her sake.
> (ll.26–7)

In spite of the rhetoric – or because of it – the highly-wrought conceit is intelligible and makes an immediate impact on the reader. Narrative takes up only the first third of the poem and ends with the elliptical:

> SHE'S for the Moores, & MARTYRDOM.
> (l.63)

The preposition conveys the action here rather than the verb, a syntactic device that, because of its compression, is used in present-day newspaper headlines.

Some types of syntax are common to both narrative and rhapsodic poems. Crashaw often manages with few connectives. In this he is somewhat similar to Herbert, although the resulting texture is less dense and the meaning immediately clearer than that of many of Herbert's poems. 'Vpon the Bleeding Crucifix' is an example. The following stanza contains just one subordinating conjunction:

> Thy restlesse feet now cannot goe
> For vs & our eternall good,
> As they were euer wont. What though?
> They swimme. Alas, in their own floud.
> (11.13–16)

The elliptical question *What though?* is typical. In the entire poem of forty-two lines there are only seven subordinating and seven co-ordinating conjunctions connecting clauses. In addition there are three *that* clauses, two at least of which introduce postmodifications of nouns. Two of the seven subordinating conjunctions are used as part of a figurative device, facilitating a chiastic repetition of two very short clauses:

> It giues though bound; though bound 'tis free.
> (1.20)

This asyndetic style is quite common in Crashaw's verse.

In order to facilitate this type of writing Crashaw has to resort to various resumptive devices. One that occurs occasionally in *Sospetto d'Herode* is a resumptive relative:

> He saw Heav'n blossome with a new-borne light,
> On which, as on a glorious stranger gaz'd
> The Golden eyes of Night: whose Beame made bright
> The way to *Beth'lem*, and as boldly blaz'd,
> (Nor askt leave of the Sun) by Day as Night.
> By whom has Heavn's illustrious Hand-maid) rais'd
> > Three kings (or what is more) three Wise men went
> > Westward to find the worlds true *Orient*.
> > (11.129–36)

The last two of the three relative clauses, which refer back to the *new-borne light*, are both resumptive to some degree. The second is most clearly Miltonic. The first clause in this stanza, *He saw*, is a resumptive device that Crashaw uses both in this poem and others. It is part of a series of repeated syntactical frames. This particular sequence starts with the resumptive words in the middle of the clause after a prepositioned complement:

> Heavens Golden-winged Herald, late hee saw
> To a poore *Galilean* virgin sent.
> (11.97–8)

Hee saw is repeated in the second part of the stanza and thereafter comes a further eight times. Another of these repeated sentence frames is a nominal subject *that* clause:

> That hee whom the Sun serves, should faintly peepe
> Through clouds of Infant flesh; that hee the old
> Eternall word should bee a Child, and weepe.
> That hee who made the fire, should fear the cold.
> (11.177–80)

This frame occurs ten times. The repeated subject clauses are gathered up and re-stated in *These* at the end of the sequence when the statement is completed:

> These are the knotty Riddles, whose darke doubt
> Intangles his lost Thoughts, past getting out.
> (11.191–2)

This kind of resumption also occurs in the 'rhapsodic' poems, as in *Charitas Nimia*, in which the frame *still would* ... is repeated over ten lines:

> Still would The youthfull SPIRITS sing;
> And still thy spatious Palace ring.
> Still would those beauteous ministers of light
> Burn all as bright,
>
> And bow their flaming heads before thee
> Still thrones & Dominations would adore thee
> Still would those euer-wakefull sons of fire
> Keep warm thy prayse
> Both nights & dayes,
> And teach thy lou'd name to their noble lyre.
> (11.19–28)

This poem makes much use of this type of resumption with repeated questions: *What was...?* and *What did...?* occurring later.
  Closely related to repetition of syntactical frames is a kind of resumption that picks up a word from a previous clause and repeats it at the beginning of the next, a type of *anadiplosis*. An example occurs in 'The Hymn of Sainte Thomas':

> Ah this way bend thy benign floud
> To'a bleeding Heart that gaspes for *blood*.
> That *blood*, whose least drops soueraign be
> To wash my worlds of sins from me.
>   (11.47–50) [my italics]

Another, perhaps nearer to *anaphora*, comes in 'Christes sufferinges':

> I left my glorious Fathers star-pau'd Court
> E're *borne* was banish't: *borne* was glad t'embrace
> A poor (yea scarce a) roofe ...
>   (11.14–16) [my italics]

Sometimes the resumption involves a word from further back than the previous clause. *Cheeks* and *eyes* are picked up in the second stanza in this extract from 'The Weeper':

> Well does the May that lyes
> Smiling in thy *cheeks* confesse
> The April in thine *eyes*.
> Mutuall sweetnesse they expresse.
> No April ere lent kinder showres,
> Nor May return'd more faithfull flowres.
>
> O *cheeks!* Bedds of chast loues
> By your own showres seasonably dash't.
> *Eyes!* nests of milky doues
> In your own wells decently washt.
>   (11.79–88) [my italics]

Like other metaphysical poets, Crashaw is much given to ellipsis and elliptical constructions. Some have been noted already. One of these, Crashaw's habit of omitting verbs, can be demonstrated from *Vexilla Regis*:

> Larg throne of loue! Royally spred
> With purple of too Rich a red.
>   Thy crime is too much duty;
>   Thy Burthen, too much beauty;
> Glorious or Greiuous more? thus to make good
> Thy costly excellence with thy KING'S own BLOOD.
>   (11.24–30)

There is only one finite verb in this stanza: *is* and an infinitive: *to make good*. *Glorious or Greiuous more?* is very similar to *What though* in 'Vpon the Bleeding Crucifix'. This terse form of expression is found all through Crashaw's verse. Another example, in which the omitted verb has to be 'understood' from the previous clause, is from 'The Mother of Sorrowes':

> O teach those wounds to bleed
> In me; me, so to read
> This book of loues ...
>   (11.51–3)

Possibly the most elliptical – it is also an extremely abstruse clause – occurs in 'Christes sufferinges'. Christ is the speaker in the poem and explores the mystery of being seen by Herod as a threat when only a weak child, and at the same time not being recognized by the Jews as their Messiah:

> A riddle! (father) still acknowledg'd thine
> Am still refus'd; before the Infant Shrine
> Of my weake feet the Persian Magi lay
> And left their Mithra for my star: this they.
>
> But Isaacks issue the peculiar heyres,
> Of thy old goodnesse, know thee not for theires.
>   (11.35–40)

The elliptically appositive clause, realized wholly by two pronominal pro-forms: *this they*, is the turning point of the 'riddle'. The Magi forsook their religion for Christ's: *this they*, but the Jews, *Isaaks issue*, refused to recognize their own God.

Conversely, however, Crashaw occasionally uses a circumlocution, as in 'A Hymne of the Nativity':

> WELCOME, though not to those gay flyes.
> Guilded ith' Beames of earthly kings;
> Slippery soules in smiling eyes.
> (11.91–3)

The final line here, although circumlocutory, is also compressed: it conjures up a brief but vivid picture of the type of courtier one is likely to find at court. Such small and unobtrusive touches are not uncommon in Crashaw and the reader has to be constantly aware lest some significance is overlooked.

Finally, a feature of Crashaw's style in which he differs from other metaphysical poets is the length of some of his nominal groups. Some from *Sospetto d'Herode* are: *hee whom the Sun serves*; *the Great Angell-blinding light* and *This mortall enemy to mankinds good*. Most have lengthening in the postmodification as would be expected, although many have more premodifiers than the nominal groups of Donne or Herbert. This may reflect Crashaw's greater use of adjectives. The first group here has a clause postmodifying the head and the last a prepositional phrase. Other groups occur as complements or prepositional complements. Examples are: *The horrid summe of his intentions*; *the momentary wing/ Of lightning* and *Pale proofe of her fell presence*. Equally long and complex nominal groups can be found in the 'rhapsodic' verse: *this GREAT mornings mighty Busynes*; *the KEY of her huge chest/ Of Heauns*; *The Aiery Shop of soul-appeasing Sound*; *the loue-crowned Doores of this Illustrious Day* and *All the store/ Of SWEETS you haue*, all from 'To the Name of Iesus'. Similar examples may be found in most poems.

Like Herbert's, Crashaw's writing is almost completely metaphorical and, again, like Herbert's, it is frequently emblematic. An example that shows the emblematic character of his metaphor comes in 'New Year's Day', the feast of the Circumcision:

> Of all the fair-cheek't flowrs that fill thee
> None so fair thy bosom strowes,
> As this modest maiden lilly
> Our sins haue sham' d into a rose.
> (11.9–12)

The first two lines are metaphorical; the second pair add the emblematic quality of the *lilly* and the *rose*, referring respectively to the delicate whiteness of the infant Christ's flesh and to the blood spilt in the act of circumcision. Crashaw tends towards this sort of imagery even more than Herbert and, whereas Herbert's metaphor becomes almost physically literal, Crashaw's has another sort of literality, which often moves into a visionary dimension. The poem 'On the Assumption' is of this type:

> Hark! she is call'd, the parting houre is come.
> Take thy Farewell, poor world! heaun must goe home.
> A peice of heau'nly earth; Purer & brighter
> Then the chast starres, whose choise lamps come
>   to light her
> While through the crystall orbes, clearer then they
> She climbes; and makes a farre more milkey way.
> (11.1–6)

These opening lines of the poem bear some resemblance to Donne's *The Second Anniversarie*, 'The Progress of the Soul', but Crashaw's is a far more 'realistic', as well as shorter, journey through the heavens. The abstract progress of Donne's soul is quite different from the concrete details and the erotic image expressed in the final clause here. Again, this is typical of the emblem tradition.

It is partly the concreteness of Crashaw's language that accounts for occasional discordant images that have sometimes been criticized. The best-known examples, of which the following is one, come in 'The Weeper':

> And now where're he strayes,
> Among the Galilean mountaines,
> Or more vnwellcome wayes,
> He's follow'd by two faithfull fountaines;
> Two walking baths; two weeping motions;
> Portable, & compendious oceans.
> (11.145–50)

Part of the difficulty lies in the visual nature of this stanza. It is undoubtedly intended to be emblematic but emblems are visual representations of ideas and here the visual element seems to encroach too far. The circumstantial details of the setting and the dynamic or activity verbs *follow'd* and *walking* make it virtually impossible for present-day readers not to understand this as description rather than as symbolism. Furthermore, although none of the words has changed in meaning since the seventeenth century, the actual objects or associative objects have changed. In Crashaw's time the word *baths* would not have called to mind our modern sanitary-ware, nor was *portable* associated with machines such as television sets and typewriters. The choice of the Latinate words *portable* and *compendious* in collocation with the homely image of the *bath* is also unfortunate and would seem to be a breach of decorum even when Crashaw wrote the poem. If the adjectives are too elevated, the concrete noun is too homely. How far the associations of these words would have seemed ludicrous to seventeenth-century readers is now impossible to say. One of Quarles's emblems depicts *Anima* as a fountain with streams of water spurting from her upraised hands, while in the sky an angel pours water from a bottle into the head of another seated figure. The motto, a paraphrase of Jeremiah IX.1, reads: 'O! that mine Eyes, like Fountains, would begin/ To stream with Tears proportion'd to my Sin'.[7] The emblems themselves would probably have been acceptable, but the descriptive nature of the stanza still seems obtrusive. A too great use of language that evokes an indiscriminate response from the senses probably lies at the bottom of most of Crashaw's less happy images.

Crashaw uses much alliteration. The liquid /l/ is one of his most frequently alliterating sounds, as in the first stanza of *Vexilla Regis*:

   Look vp, languishing Soul! Lo where the fair
  BADG of thy faith calls back thy care,
    And biddes thee ne're forget
    Thy life is one long Debt
  Of loue to Him, who on this painfull TREE
  Paid back the flesh he took for thee.
          (11.1–6)

The initial /l/ runs almost through the whole stanza and is reinforced by other /l/ sounds which are not at the beginnings of words. Other consonants alliterate incidentally: /f/; /b/; /k/ and finally /p/. Certain sounds seem to attract Crashaw more than others, although his range is wide. Phrases such as *starry Stranger* and *rich a red* have a magic of their own. In 'To the Name of Iesus', in which music is invoked, Crashaw makes play with /m/ and other nasals:

> Help me to meditate mine Immortall Song.
> Come, ye soft ministers of sweet sad mirth.
> (11.61–2)

At times, Crashaw uses alliteration to reinforce the sense and focus attention on an important point; at others he seems to delight in sound for its own sake. Unquestionably he had a good ear for the music of poetry. This is apparent in the secular poem 'Musick's Duell', published in *The Delights of the Muses* (1646). His alertness to the scope of word music extends beyond mere alliteration to medial and final consonants and also to vowel sounds. One stanza from 'The Weeper' will show how he uses sound to conjure up a sensuous image that is both aural and visual:

> The deaw no more will weep
> The primrose's pale cheek to deck,
> The deaw no more will sleep
> Nuzzel'd in the lilly's neck;
> Much reather would it be thy TEAR,
> And leaue them Both to tremble here.
> (11.43–8)

The sounds of the words *cheek to deck* require little physiological adjustment of the speech organs and sound correspondingly close to the ear. The *ch* /tʃ/ of *cheek* is a dental which is near to /d/ of *deck*. Similarly, the long /i:/ of *cheek* is a high vowel and is slightly lowered in /e/ of *deck*. Both the consonants and vowels that change are front sounds; only the final /k/ is a back consonant. The fourth line has a chiastic repetition of consonants that makes a satisfying aural pattern:

> n   z   l   / /   l   z   n

Again the /ɪ/ vowels of *lilly's* are high front vowels, short this time, and are lowered in the /e/ of *neck*. In addition there is almost exact repetition of the first and third lines, which contributes to the other combinations of sound. Much of Crashaw's verse could be analysed to show the different 'tunes' he plays.

An occasional simile can be found in the narrative verse, although the constant metaphor leaves little room for simile. In *Sospetto d'Herode* there is a description of Satan's wings:

> Hee shooke himselfe, and spread his spatious wings:
> Which like two Bosom'd sailes embrace the dimme
>   Aire, with a dismall shade.
> (11.141–3)

Others occur in connection with the visit of the Erinnys, the Furies of classical mythology, to Herod. One, in speaking to him, uses a simile of almost epic length:

> So sleeps a Pilot, whose poore Barke is prest
> With many a mercylesse o're mastring wave;
> For whom (as dead) the wrathfull winds contest,
> Which of them deep'st shall digge her watry Grave.
> (11.425–8)

As in Herbert, and later in Vaughan, so in Crashaw's verse references to biblical events occur everywhere. Unlike Herbert, however, and far more than Donne, Crashaw alludes to classical figures. This is especially so in *Sospetto d'Herode*, in which most of Satan's minions are from classical mythology. Even here, Crashaw mixes biblical and classical allusions indiscriminately: in one line we find *Medaea* consorting with *Jezabell* as two of the 'most abhorred Maids of Honour' (1.337) of the fourth Fury, or Erinnys, otherwise called Cruelty. Personifications are likewise freely scattered in this part of the poem: *Hate*; *Wrath*; *Rage*; *Famine* and so on. Crashaw pays scant heed to historical accuracy and Nero takes his place in this poem set in the days of Caesar Augustus, several years before Nero's birth. Old and New Testament stories are also combined, but for this, of course, there is good precedent in the New Testament itself. 'Vpon the Bleeding Crucifix', for example, describes the blood of Christ in terms of the Flood:

> This thy blood's deluge, a dire chance,
> Dear LORD to Thee, to vs is found
> A deluge of Deliuerance;
> A deluge least we should be drown'd.
>
> (11.37–40)

The riddling element in this last quotation is typical of Crashaw, as of the other metaphysical poets. Apart from metaphor and word play, paradox and riddling are the most frequent features of Crashaw's figurative language. There is constant juxtaposition of 'day' and 'night', 'light' and 'darkness', usually in connection with Christ. This is particularly so in 'A Hymne of the Nativity':

> The BABE look't vp and shew'd his Face;
> In spite of Darknes, it was DAY.
> It was THY day, SWEET! & did rise
> Not from the EAST but from thine EYES.
>
> (11.19–22)

In this poem there is the paradoxical concept of the infinite contained not only in the finite, but a finite that is small enough for man to comprehend:

> Wellcome, all WONDERS in one sight!
> AEternity shutt in a span.
> Sommer in Winter. Day in Night.
> Heauen in earth, & GOD in MAN.
>
> (11.79–82)

Immediately before is the kind of antithetical word play, used by most of the metaphysical poets:

> Great little one! whose all-embracing birth
> Lifts earth to heauen, stoopes heau'n to earth.
>
> (11.83–4)

The same type of paradox comes in 'The Flaming Heart'. In this poem Crashaw's frequent exploitation of sexual images is most fully realized. He argues that Teresa should be depicted with the male attribute ('that fiery DART') that the painting gives to the Seraphim. At the end he declares that the wound the saint receives is itself a sufficiently masculine instrument. The sexual implication underlies the paradox of the following lines:

> For in loue's feild was neuer found
> A nobler weapon then a WOVND.
> Loue's passiues are his actiu'st part.
> The wounded is the wounding heart.
> (11.71–4)

It seems that Teresa's agony, which delights even as it wounds, arouses in the poet a desire for a similar experience. Thus, her passivity becomes active in affecting others with its own intoxication.[8] Such paradoxes are central to Crashaw's thought and are not always easy to understand, or, if we can perceive their deeper meaning, they are certainly not easy to elucidate in plain prose. The central paradox of the Christian religion is stated in a neatly turned couplet in *O Gloriosa Domina*:

> He that made all things, had not done
> Till he had made Himself thy son.
> (11.5–6)

Crashaw looks so intently at what he has to say that he willingly takes the most striking way of saying it even if, in so doing, he risks being fantastic or over sensuous for many people's taste. The 'baroque' nature of his language may be less readily accessible to some English readers than that of other metaphysical poets. His poetry appears extravagant, lacking in the chaste native style that we associate with Herbert. Nevertheless, it can and often does reach heights that thrill the imagination with daring. Once his particular manner of writing is accepted, it is clear that his finely-wrought language is as fitting for its subject matter as that of any other religious poet of the period.

5 Henry Vaughan (1621–95)

> '*a great* Ring *of pure and endless light*'
> ('I saw Eternity')

The language of Vaughan's religious poems is probably more varied and eclectic than that of the other metaphysical poets. Direction and meaning may often seem unclear and diffuse. It is not surprising, therefore, that critics disagree about the nature, intentions and quality of his poetry.

Vaughan's world view in *Silex Scintillans* (1650 and 1655) is a blend of hermetic philosophy and Christian doctrine, especially that of the Bible. He infers correspondences between all levels of creation, a 'sympathy' that binds all things together and the world to its Creator in a single whole. God's harmony is broken only by man, who by restlessness and lack of direction disrupts the pattern and introduces discord. Man seeks salvation and rest and these he pursues in a series of advances towards and retreats from his Maker. If he perseveres, he ultimately returns to God. This, simplified, is Vaughan's philosophy and it is reflected in the language of his poetry and is the key to his linguistic usage.[1]

The way in which Vaughan's thought is reflected in language shows most clearly in his imagery. Belief in correspondences between various levels of being, which was an essential part of hermetic philosophy, leads to certain types of figurative expression: symbolism, allegory, metaphor and simile. Vaughan scatters such figures throughout his verse. The opening poem of *Silex Scintillans*, 'Regeneration', is full of them:

>   at last
>   'Twixt steps, and falls
> I reach'd the pinacle, where plac'd
>   I found a paire of scales.
>   (11.17–20)

A pair of scales was, of course, a traditional emblem and survives today as a symbol of justice. If the reader has not already understood that the speaker of the poem is not moving through a natural landscape, this stanza makes it clear. 'Regeneration' progresses through a series of such emblems or symbols. They may not all be immediately recognized as such: a field, a grove, a fountain, a bank of flowers, a 'rushing wind'. The last, by reason of its premodifying adjective, is readily identified as biblical in origin (Acts 11.2). Emblematic imagery is everywhere, as in the *Primros'd* shade in the first stanza.[2] Not all of Vaughan's poems contain as many symbols as 'Regeneration' but there are many of them. 'The Search' begins:

> 'Tis now cleare day: I see a Rose
> Bud in the bright East, and disclose
> The Pilgrim-Sunne.
>   (11.1–3)

The symbolic 'Rose' and its association with dawn is readily grasped. What sort of dawn is less clear. In collocation with the title of the poem and the *Pilgrim-Sunne* it seems to prefigure the discovery with which the search will end. The rosy sky denotes sunrise, but in the context of this poem it also heralds a false dawn. As often, Vaughan's symbols here are more private than those of earlier poets; he loosens and widens the traditional references of images. For this reason his use of emblems is not so obvious, but any doubt that he was consciously following the emblem tradition is dispelled by the title page of the 1650 edition of *Silex Scintillans*. This shows an engraving of a hand reaching from heaven to strike fire from a rock-like heart, which at the same time weeps tears. The use of a colour adjective in the first line of 'The Search' – it is the colour of the sky that is evoked – as a noun is typical of Vaughan (see p.117). Here it denotes the flower, which allows Vaughan to extend the symbolic use of language to include the verb *Bud*. The use is ambivalent but vivid, and stirs the imagination with sensations that seem just beyond conscious thought. It is both allusive and elusive.

Many of Vaughan's poems can be read on more than one level throughout. Their language is partly emblematic, partly allegorical. The allegory is not always sustained and shifts within the course of a single poem, as in 'The Proffer':

> Be still black Parasites,
>   Flutter no more;
> Were it still winter, as it was before,
>   You'd make no flights;
> But now the dew and Sun have warm'd my bowres,
>   You flie and flock to suck the flowers.
>   (11.1–6)

The allegory of the bees, an emblem modified from traditional sources, runs through three stanzas and then the poem moves on to other more fragmentary allusions, all serving to illustrate the wisdom of rejecting worldly preferment and flattery and keeping one's sights fixed on heavenly rewards. In 'I walkt the other day', one of a group of elegiac poems, the allegory is sustained throughout the poem, which is complex and has several possible interpretations. It opens on a disarmingly casual and literal level:

> I walkt the other day (to spend my hour)
>   Into a field
> Where I sometimes had seen the soil to yield
>   A gallant flowre ...
>   (11.1–4)

The walk, however, is more than it at first seems. It is a visit to a grave (probably that of the poet's younger brother, William) and the 'gallant flowre' is a young man who has died. This second layer of meaning is soon disclosed:

> Then taking up what I could neerest spie
>   I digg'd about
> That place where I had seen him to grow out,
>   And by and by
> I saw the warm Recluse alone to lie
>   Where fresh and green
> He lived of us unseen.
>   (11.15–21)

The apparent strangeness is partly caused by the masculine pronoun *he*, which seems to denote a person but which also directly refers to the 'gallant flowre'. Vaughan often makes inanimate objects masculine or sometimes feminine.[3] At this point the reader is likely to be alerted to the spiritual pitch of the poem. The allegorical expression is plainly stated in the penultimate stanza:

> That in these Masques and shadows I may see
> > Thy sacred way,
> And by those hid ascents climb to that day
> > Which breaks from thee
> Who art in all things, though invisibly.
> > > (11.50–4)

The full meaning is elusive and multivalent but one facet of it is given in this stanza: that God permeates the universe and dwells in each separate piece of his creation.

Allegory is a kind of sustained metaphor and metaphorical language is implicit in most of Vaughan's poems. However, he also uses straightforward metaphors and these, too, inevitably suggest correspondences between different things. Life is seen as a thoroughfare in 'The Ass':

> > this busie street
> Of flesh and blood.
> > (11.1–2)

In 'Sure, there's a tye of Bodyes!' man himself is

> such a Marygold ...
> > That shuts, and hangs the head.
> > > (11.7–8)

The night is metaphorically represented by many things in the poem of that title:

> > this worlds defeat;
> The stop to busie fools; cares check and curb;
> The day of Spirits; my souls calm retreat
> > Which none disturb!
> *Christs* progress, and his prayer time;
> The hours to which high Heaven doth chime.
> > > (11.26–30)

This particular succession of metaphors is an example of *dyfalu*, a Welsh poetical device, in which comparisons are listed and multiplied. Herbert also uses this device. Vaughan makes use of it again in 'Son-dayes'. A metaphor, reflecting man's restlessness, in which Vaughan uses domestic-type imagery similar to Herbert's, is:

> Man is the shuttle, to whose winding quest
> And passage through these looms
> God order'd motion, but ordain'd no rest.
> ('Man', 11.26–8)

Metaphor here is neatly extended through three lines.

Simile, or explicit metaphor, occurs frequently. Two short examples, both characteristically making natural phenomena the objects of comparison, are:

> ... men might look and live as Glo-worms shine;
> ('The Night', 1.3)

and:

> my thoughts shal move
> Like Bees in storms unto their Hive.
> ('The Obsequies', 11.29–30)

Many of Vaughan's similes are long and involve extended parallelism. One poem that clearly demonstrates this is 'The Pilgrimage', which is wholly made up of two such similes, each followed by one stanza of further comment. A less lengthy but still extended simile, involving the medicinal properties of plants, comes in 'Death':

> As harmless violets, which give
>   Their virtues here
> For salves and syrups, while they live,
> Do after calmly disappear,
> And neither grieve, repine, nor fear:
>
> So dye his servants; and as sure
>   Shall they revive.
>   (11.21–7)

Word play and paradox, which make up such a large part of the figurative language of Donne and Herbert, are rarely used by Vaughan. An occasional instance occurs in the first book of *Silex Scintillans*. One from 'Distraction' is:

>   Hadst thou
> Made me a starre, a pearle, or a rain-bow,
>   The beames I then had shot
>   My light had lessend not,
>   But now
> I find my selfe the lesse, the more I grow.
>   (11.5–10)

Another area in which Vaughan pursues his search for correspondences is sound. The seeming casualness of his rhymes has often been noted but most instances are near rhymes, wholly acceptable in Welsh poetry.[4] Examples of near rhymes are: *fear* rhymed with *there*; *speak* with *break* and *stones* with *once*, all from 'The Stone'. In the same poem Vaughan also rhymes *word* and *world*. Near rhymes are frequent throughout Vaughan's poetry. He also uses a sort of assonantal echo, in which the final consonants or consonant clusters are close in sound and the preceding vowels are the same: *husk* and *dust* ('The Pursuit'); *sins* and *limbs* (' The Passion'); *slipped* and *pit* ('The Relapse') and *groves* and *grows* ('Religion'). Otherwise, Vaughan's rhymes are conventional and some of the so-called defective rhymes would have been good rhymes in the English pronunciation – and possibly even more so in the Welsh pronunciation of English – of his day.

Apart from rhyme, Vaughan uses all the devices of alliteration, assonance[5] and what Hopkins called 'consonantal chime'. This last appears in Welsh poetry in various complex but regulated forms as *cynghanedd* and may have been familiar to Vaughan from his reading of Welsh literature. Alliteration occurs everywhere in the poems. Sometimes it is confined to doublets or two or three words, as in *wind and water* and *wash and wing* in 'The Storm' and *cares check and curb* in 'The Night'. Elsewhere, there is more extended alliteration. In 'The Proffer' (11.2–6) quoted above (p.102) the /fl/ sound is repeated through five lines. An interweaving of alliterative consonants occurs in 'The Water-fall':

> With what deep murmurs through times silent stealth
> Doth thy transparent, cool and watry wealth
>   Here flowing fall,
>   And chide, and call,
> As if his liquid, loose Retinue staid
> Lingring ...
>
> (11.1–6)

The /w/ sounds of the initial words are picked up in *watry wealth* at the end of the second line. There is alliteration of /s/ and /f/, and the underlying /l/ sound that runs through the first three lines finally surfaces in the alliteration of *liquid, loose* followed by *Lingring*. This is approaching 'consonantal chime'. The continuation of the /l/ alliteration into the following line, followed by the caesura, conveys the sense of the water momentarily suspended on the brink before it tumbles over into the fall itself. Assonance, the repetition of vowel sounds, is rarer and certainly less obvious than alliteration but not infrequent. It almost always occurs in conjunction with one of the consonantal types of repetition, as in:

> Gods silent, searching flight.
> ('The Night', 1.31)

The /aɪ/ of *silent* is repeated in *flight*. In addition, both words contain /l/ and /t/ and, although not alliterating, the initial fricative of *flight* echoes the fricative /s/ of *silent, searching*.

Vaughan's diffuseness and complexity extend to vocabulary. The multivalency and allusive quality of the words he uses reflect his attempt to bring the variety of a creation beyond reckoning into a whole, a circle or 'ring'.

Like Herbert, Vaughan uses many everyday words and much colloquial vocabulary. However, words denoting household objects themselves (although he has a fair sprinkling of these) do not dominate his verse as they do Herbert's. It is in the way he uses everyday words that Vaughan's own distinctive voice is heard. He juxtaposes colloquial and other types of words and it is the juxtaposition, characteristic of the whole tenor of Vaughan's verse, that often gives his vocabulary its particular impact. In 'Faith' we find these lines describing the coming of day:

> Stars shut up shop, mists pack away,
> And the Moon mourns.
> (11.19–20)

Shut up shop was a common idiom at the time but is surprising in collocation with *stars*. *Pack away* is not listed in the *OED* but Thomas Heywood has the same form of the verb, used intransitively, as here, in his poem which begins with the exhortation, 'Pack, clouds, away' (c.1605). The verb was, therefore, in use at the time. The colloquial quality of these phrasal verbs is unmistakeable and such verbs are frequent. In the following line, however, the language shifts from the register of the market place. The two words *Moon* and *mourns* vary only in the medial vowel, with a marginal retroflex /r/ in *mourns*. The drawn-out nasals and long vowel sounds, as well as the semantic associations of the two words, lift the clause to a lyrical plane. This contrasts directly with the perky, staccato effects of the alliteration, the final consonantal stops, /t/ and /p/, and the short vowels in *Shut up shop*.

The simple language which Vaughan uses sometimes reaches heights which Herbert's rarely achieves. This may be because of the various ways in which Vaughan places the simple and the complex or unusual side by side. The *dyfalu* (list of appositive comparisons) in 'The Night' contains several such evocative phrases:

> Gods silent, searching flight:
> When my Lords head is fill'd with dew, and all
> His locks are wet with the clear drops of night;
> His still, soft call;
> His knocking time.
>
> (11.31–5)

The *still, soft call*, echoing the biblical 'still small voice' (II Kings IX.12), makes its impact by contrasting simple monosyllabic words with the strangeness of the highly-wrought conceit in the previous two lines.[6] This is also realized in monosyllabic words mainly of native stock. The nominal group in the final line contains equally simple, commonly used words but the meaning is compressed. Once understood, the strength of the image thrills the imagination. We saw that Crashaw also makes large statements in simple words. Vaughan's 'The Incarnation, and Passion' affords one instance of an overwhelming truth conveyed in everyday words of native origin:

> To put on Clouds instead of light,
> And cloath the morning-starre with dust.
> (11.5–6)

The reader experiences a strange excitement, which is the result of the contrast of the simple language and the vastness of the concept it expresses. The distance between *morning-starre* and *dust* is breath-taking. Such visionary glimpses have earned Vaughan the name of mystic. Hutchinson says that any of the metaphysical poets could have written the two lines just quoted but it was Vaughan who did.[7]

The word *light* is one of Vaughan's favourite words and others denoting various kinds of light (and darkness) abound. Not only words but whole expressions and lines indicate different sorts of light and the effects of light and shade. The stones in the fountain in 'Regeneration'

> as quick as light
> Danc'd through the floud;
> (11.57–8)

the darkness in 'The Night' is *deep, but dazling*; and at dawn

> The whole Creation shakes off night,
> And for thy shadow looks the light.
> ('The Dawning' 11.17–18)

One of Vaughan's best-known poems begins:

> They are all gone into the world of light!
> And I alone sit lingring here.
> (11.1–2)

The poem continues with images drawn from light until the enigmatic lines of the third stanza:

> I see them walking in an Air of glory,
>   Whose light doth trample on my days:
> My days, which are at best but dull and hoary,
>   Meer glimering and decays.
> (11.9–12)

In almost every poem Vaughan refers to light in some way, often in a simile or other image. The *Scintillans* of the title is well justified. The whole sequence of poems radiates light.

Many critics have noted Vaughan's predilection for the colour adjectives *white* and *green*. *White* is often associated with 'light' imagery, especially in the elegiac group of poems. In 'As time one day by me did pass' the mourner sees the name of the person who has died in time's book:

> in
> A fair, white page of thin
> And ev'n smooth lines, like the Suns rays.
> (11.9-11)

A visionary light, common to this group, runs through the poem and is interwoven with references to both *white*, the colour of innocence and purity, and *green*, symbolic of rebirth and growth. The speaker also sees:

> In the same page thy humble grave
> Set with green herbs ...
> (11.23-4)

and finally he foresees the certainty of new life arising from death's ashes:

> In deaths dark mysteries
> A beauty far more bright
> Then the noons cloudless light
> For whose dry dust green branches bud
> And robes are bleach'd in the *Lambs* blood.
> (11.32-6)

Blood has a cleansing power and so is associated with the white of bleaching rather than the sacrificial *red*, so often found in Crashaw's poetry. *Red* usually denotes evil and negative things in Vaughan, as in 'Abels Blood', where both *purple* and *red* are used of the first murder. *White* is a colour word which Vaughan also shares with Crashaw, although Crashaw uses it surprisingly infrequently and much more sensuously. *Green*, a cool colour related to the natural world of growing plants, is in direct contrast to the rather hothouse atmosphere created by Crashaw's colour imagery. It is significant that in his rendering of Psalm CIV.16 Vaughan introduces *green* in the line 'Thou giv'st the trees their greenness' (1.45). It does not appear in the Bible version.[8] Altogether Vaughan makes more sparing use of colours and colour imagery than Crashaw but his use repays attention.

Another important source of Vaughan's vocabulary is nature. Chiefly through nature words and the contexts in which he places them, Vaughan demonstrates the correspondences that unite creation into one 'sympathetic' whole. Three types of nature vocabulary can be distinguished.

First, there is a freshness about Vaughan's nature images and language that stems from his interest in nature and herbal medicine. This is rare in the mid-seventeenth century and it is possibly the first time that it happens consistently in English religious poetry. It is worth remembering that Izaak Walton, who wrote the first biographies of both Donne and Herbert, also wrote *The Compleat Angler*. It was published in 1653, the exact time that Vaughan was busy with *Silex Scintillans*. Walton's work, too, has an 'outdoor' atmosphere that is comparable in some ways with Vaughan's poetry. Vaughan, we feel, writes from first-hand observation. When he says in 'Thou that know'st for whom I mourne':

> Yet have I knowne thy slightest things
>   A *feather*, or a *shell*,
> A *stick* or *Rod*, which some Chance brings
>   The best of us excell,
>   (11.21–4)

we believe that he had both looked at and pondered on the objects named. How does he achieve this sense of conviction? First, the rhythm is leisurely. Each four-foot iambic line is followed by one of three feet, which makes for a slightly longer pause at the end of the shorter line. The second object named, the *shell*, falls at the end of one of these shorter lines, while the last, the *Rod*, comes before the caesura of the following line. All four objects succeed one another without intervening comment or description. They are presented starkly. There is no modification, apart from the three indefinite articles. Nothing distracts attention from the things named. On the other hand, each pair is separated by the co-ordinator *or*. This allows the reader to linger over each object in turn (the rhythmic pauses after *shell* and *Rod* have been explained) and conveys the impression that the writer also pauses to reflect on their significance. Although Vaughan uses many striking adjectives to premodify nouns, he also presents the reader with words of significance (not always nouns) in this unvarnished way. This is one of the methods by which he convinces us that he is writing from direct observation. Descriptions, involving participles and adjectives, can have a similar effect. An example from 'The Water-fall' is:

> As this loud brooks incessant fall
> In streaming rings restagnates all,
> Which reach by course the bank, and then
> Are no more seen ...
> (11.33–6)

The unusual Latinate form *restagnates* slightly obscures the picture but the movement of the falling water is accurately caught. Another natural phenomenon, the flickering movement of fire, is vividly described in 'Misery':

> As flames about their fuel run
> And work, and wind til all be done.
> (11.77–8)

Vaughan almost always depicts natural things in movement. This mirrors the hermetic belief in a world endlessly changing and being transmuted into new forms and substances. There is a clear example of this cyclical aspect of nature in the first stanza of 'The Showre':

> 'Twas so, I saw thy birth: That drowsie Lake
> From her faint bosome breath'd thee, the disease
> Of her sick waters, and Infectious Ease.
>   But, now at Even
>   Too grosse for heaven,
> Thou fall'st in teares, and weep'st for thy mistake.
> (11.1–6)

The language is more literary but the natural process is again accurately observed.

The second aspect of Vaughan's nature language is classical and literary. 'Mount of Olives' (I) is a poem ostensibly about a biblical subject but Vaughan names two English hills, *Cotswold* and *Coopers*,⁹ and then continues:

> both have met
> With learned swaines, and Eccho yet
> Their pipes, and wit;
> ...
> And what need
> The sheep bleat thee a silly Lay
> That heard'st both reed
> And sheepward play?
> (11.9–16)

The classical mode and stylized pastoral vocabulary stand out. *Sheepward* is an archaic form of *shepherd*. The influence of Spenser and the English pastoral tradition is clear. 'Mount of Olives' (II) is written in a similar style:

> ... I felt through all my powr's
> Such a rich air of sweets, as Evening showrs
> Fand by a gentle gale Convey and breath
> On some parch'd bank, crown'd with a flowrie wreath.
> (11.3–6)

Vocabulary and expression in this poem come near to Milton and, later, to the early poetry of Pope. Once the meaning behind the literary style is grasped, it becomes clear that Vaughan's awareness of evening scents after light rain is as acute as any of his more down-to-earth descriptions.

The third type of Vaughan's nature writing draws on the Bible and its vocabulary. He uses it not only for paraphrases of the Psalms but also in his poetry as a whole. Many biblical words, such as *valley*; *mountain*; *fragrance* and a host of others overlap with the vocabulary that appears in the English pastoral and literary tradition of the late sixteenth to eighteenth centuries. Many of these occur, more specifically, in the Song of Songs, which both attracted and influenced the metaphysical poets. In addition, the more ordinary words, such as *bird*; *bough*; *field*, and even such English-seeming specific names as *oak* and *thorn*, also occur in the Bible. The three strands of nature vocabulary are rarely separated completely in the poems. By interweaving them Vaughan again draws together various parts of his experience. It is commonly thought that he depicts nature that is natural and essentially British, although this can be disputed.[10] There are, however, some surprising juxtapositions that belie the notion that he was describing a 'natural' landscape at all. 'Regeneration' is the first and most obvious example of a landscape that seems natural but which, as the poem progresses, becomes highly stylized. Another instance is the poem 'Corruption'. In man's 'early days':

> Angels lay *Leiger* here; Each Bush, and Cel,
> Each Oke, and high-way knew them,
> Walk but the fields, or sit down at some *wel*,
> And he was sure to view them.
> (11.25–8)

Most of the nature words, including the very British-sounding *Oke*, are to be found in the Bible. The presence of the ambassadorial angels confirms that Vaughan is not attempting to present a realistic countryside. The unexpected naming of English hills in 'Mount of Olives' (I) (although these have literary sources) is part and parcel of the same mentality. This mingling of places shows that for Vaughan all his experience, topographical, philosophical and religious, including his main source of inspiration, the Bible, made up one imaginative landscape.

An important group of words in Vaughan's poetry is that connected with hermetic philosophy and particularly those denoting the divine spark or essence that is found in every object and creature. Vaughan uses many words for this and it is necessary to recognize when one is being used in order to grasp his full meaning. Some of them are *grain*; *seed*; *essence* itself; *signature*; *spice* and *dew*. The last two are also biblical – they are used in the Song of Songs. *Blood* is also sometimes included. Other words, more often used in the accepted sense, clearly signify, in some poems, the divine essence. Conversely, the words cited above are sometimes used with their ordinary meanings and do not have this particular connotation. An example of words indicating the divine essence are *Ray* and *grain* in 'Repentance':

> Lord, since thou didst in this vile Clay
>   That sacred Ray
> Thy spirit plant, quickning the whole
> With that one grains Infused wealth,
> My forward flesh creept on, and subtly stole
> Both growth, and power ...
>   (11.1–6)

In this case, however, the divine spark is initially perverted by man. The opening of the often quoted 'Cock-crowing' contains a number of these words and also phrases denoting the same thing. They include *Sunnie seed*; *glance of day*; *grain* and *Ray* again; *candle*; *tincture* and *touch*. The word *magnetisme* also occurs and is related in meaning to what Vaughan elsewhere calls 'the tye of Bodyes'. The rather more unusual and technical word *signature* also occurs in 'Repentance':

> The drops of rain, the sighs of wind,
> The Stars to which I am stark blind,
> The Dew thy herbs drink up by night,
> The beams they warm them at i'th'light,
> All that have signature or life ...
>   (11.37–41)

In this instance *Dew* denotes the physical phenomenon and not the spiritual essence. *Life*, it will be noted, is ascribed to all the inanimate objects named here and is equated with the essence or *signature*.

Biblical language and vocabulary are so pervasive in *Silex Scintillans* that any account of Vaughan's language would be incomplete without reference to them. They cannot be considered only in individual words, for whole lines and stanzas echo the Bible or allude to parables and quotations from it. The parable of the Prodigal Son in 'The Pursuite' is one of the more obvious examples, although the only words that Vaughan takes from St Luke's Gospel (XV.11–32) are *lost*; *Sonne* and *huske*:

> Hadst thou given to this active dust
>   A state untir'd,
> The lost Sonne had not left the huske
>   Nor home desir'd.
>   (11.9–12)

Another readily identified line, based on Paul's First Letter to the Corinthians (XIII.12), is in 'Resurrection and Immortality':

> Then I that here saw darkly in a glasse ...
>   (1.51)

It is easy to miss a partial quotation or allusion which may be the key to the meaning of a poem or part of a poem. An example of this occurs in 'The Retreate'. The child looks back to the place from which it came and the adult, remembering this, longs to retrace those first steps and:

> once more reach that plaine,
> Where first I left my glorious traine,
> From whence th' Inlightned spirit sees
> That shady City of Palme trees.
>   (11.23–6)

The 'shady City of Palme trees' might be taken by the reader for Jerusalem or the Heavenly City, the New Jerusalem. In fact, it is a direct quotation from Deuteronomy (XXXIV.1–4) and refers to Jericho.[11] Jericho lay in the heart of the Promised Land and was shown to the dying Moses from afar. This makes the allusion peculiarly poignant for, just as Moses was never to reach the Promised Land, neither can man retrace his steps to Heaven, the spiritual Promised Land, during the course of his earthly journey. The word *shady* is an addition of Vaughan's and is characteristic of his awareness of the effects of light and shade. It adds a living touch to the Bible picture.

Besides words of native and Germanic origin Vaughan uses a considerable amount of Latinate and Romance vocabulary. Many of the poems which contain clusters of Romance and Latinate words are not memorable. However, Vaughan uses some uncommon words and formations from Romance sources. Among the more unusual are *resentient* ('The Timber'); *anguishments* ('The Search'); *contaction* ('Sure there's a tye of Bodyes!'); *acceptation* ('Christs Nativity') and *paisage* ('Mount of Olives' (II)).

There are many striking compound words and these are almost invariably made up of native elements. A few examples are *far-day*; *forerun*; *out-runs* (all from 'Rules *and* Lessons'); *outvie* ('Repentance'); *love-twist* ('Retirement'); *wine-house* and *self-ends* ('The Agreement') and *lively-fair* ('St Mary Magdalen').

The way in which Vaughan uses parts of speech is worth noting. His verbs are particularly forceful. They are more dynamic than is usual in metaphysical poetry. Some of the most memorable are functional shifts, usually from nouns, and they often occur in the best-known poems, such as 'The Morning-watch':

> This Dew fell on my breast;
> O how it *Blouds*,
> And *Spirits* all my Earth!
> (11.7–9)

Dew, the vital spark of hermetic philosophy, is the subject of the two active and transitive verbs, *Blouds* and *Spirits*, the latter from an abstract noun. Another example is *mist* from 'The Relapse':

> Dark as my deeds,
> Should *mist* within me, and put out that lamp
> Thy spirit feeds.
> (11.14–16)

Not only is the divine essence present in the word *lamp* but the result of the action of the verb *mist* is to obscure the vision or glimpse of the divine that Vaughan so often laments he has lost. Frequently the functional shifts take the form of a participle, usually the past participle, such as *crumm'd* in '(thus *crumm'd*) I stray' ('Buriall') and *mountain'd* in 'the *mountain'd* wave' ('The Storm'). The latter is a premodifier of the noun *wave* and one of Vaughan's many unusual adjectives.

Generally, the metaphysical poets use adjectives minimally and those that do occur are fairly pedestrian. Vaughan, like Crashaw, is something of an exception, although his adjectives are not so much striking in themselves as used in unexpected ways. At times they take on an almost substantive force from the emphasis placed on them, as at the beginning of 'The World':

> I saw Eternity the other night
> Like a great *Ring* of pure and endless light,
> All calm, as it was bright.
> (11.1–3)

These lines are among the best-known in the whole of Vaughan's poetry. The words themselves are unremarkable taken singly but together they constitute what is possibly Vaughan's most startling statement. He extracts every drop of meaning from each word, including the adjectives. *Pure* and *endless* occur in a prepositional phrase postmodifying *Ring*. Because they come after *Ring* they receive more stress than the premodifying adjective *great*. They are separated by a co-ordinator, and the spacing focuses the reader's attention on each in turn. This emphasizes the distinct meanings. *Calm* and *bright* are also separated, coming in different halves of the last line. *All calm* is a postmodifier but can also be seen as an elliptical correlative clause. The adjective falls before the caesura, coinciding with the metrical stress. It is followed by the second correlative clause that ends with the adjective *bright* in the final stressed position. Other examples of this means of drawing attention to individual words can be found. Sometimes Vaughan treats verbs in this way. An example occurs in 'The Storm':

> And *wind*, and *water* to thy use
> Both *wash*, and *wing* my soul.
> (11.23–4)

Again, the verbs are separated from each other by co-ordination and alliteration emphasizes them still further.

At least once Vaughan uses functional shift to form a striking adverb:

> Thus fed my Eyes
> But all the Eare lay hush.
> ('Regeneration' 11.47–8)

Hush is usually a noun. Another possible instance comes at the end of 'The Night':

> O for that night! where I in him
> Might live invisible and dim.
> (ll.53–4)

This is syntactically ambiguous. *Invisible* and *dim* could be adjectives postmodifying *I* or adverbs qualifying *live*. They can be taken as both at the same time.

Functional shift to nouns is usually from verbs, as with *discusse* in 'The Storm':

> But when his waters billow thus,
>   Dark storms, and wind
> Incite them to that fierce discusse;
> (ll.9–11)

and *wash* in 'The Water-fall', which the poet calls:

> My sacred wash and cleanser here.
> (l.24)

Donne also uses functional shift but not as much as Vaughan. Vaughan moves freely among the parts of speech, paying scant attention to the lines drawn between them. This is consistent with his vision of all disparities harmonized into one. Boundaries, even in language, may be broken down so that components merge in new wholes.

Vaughan's sentence types are as varied as other aspects of his language. At first his poems seem to be full of questions, exclamations and exhortations. These are generally short, often consisting of one clause only. There are many more affirmative statements, however, and many of these are long and loosely structured. Vaughan favours co-ordination but he also has much subordination.

Two characteristics of his syntax may be noted for the way in which they reflect his liking for parallels and correspondences. One is the use he makes of connectives such as *thus*; *hence* and *so*, meaning 'in this way'. With these words Vaughan makes connections and semantic parallels between statements. They are effectively similes. In 'Thou that know'st for whom I mourne' both *thus* and *hence* occur within a few lines of each other:

> Yea, I have knowne these shreds out last
>   A fair-compacted frame
> And for one *Twenty* we have past
>   Almost outlive our name.
> Thus hast thou plac'd in mans outside
>   Death to the Common Eye,
> That heaven within him might abide,
>   And close eternitie;
> Hence, youth, and folly (man's first shame,)
>   Are put unto the slaughter ...
>   (11.25-34)

The number of times *so* is used in a similar way is increased by the similes that use the correlative conjunctions *as ... so*.

An extract from '*Isaacs* Marriage' will illustrate Vaughan's loose sentence structure:

> And now thou knewest her coming, It was time
> To get thee wings on, and devoutly climbe
> Unto thy God, for Marriage of all states
> Makes most unhappy, or most fortunates;
> This brought thee forth, where now thou didst undress
> Thy soul, and with new pinions refresh
> Her wearied wings, which so restor'd did flye
> Above the stars, a track unknown, and high,
> And in her piercing flight perfum'd the ayer
> Scatt'ring the *Myrrhe*, and incense of thy pray'r.
>   (11.43-52)

The verse paragraph begins with a co-ordinate conjunction which connects it to the preceding lines, in which Isaac has just had his first sight of Rebecca. The first four lines of the paragraph constitute a complete syntactical unit. The next line begins with the word *This*, which is a deictic pronoun, but its antecedent is not clear. It seems to be the fact of Isaac's having seen Rebecca. The location of *where*, which connects the ensuing co-ordinate clauses, is also uncertain and seems to refer more to a state of mind than to a geographical place. *Which* (1.49) initiates a non-restrictive relative clause but this time the antecedent is clearly *Her wearied wings*. The included participle clause: *so restor'd*, is an instance of the compressed syntax that Vaughan occasionally uses. It is really a postmodifier of *Her wearied wings*. In the following co-ordinate relative clause the prepositional phrase: *in her piercing flight* indicates that the antecedent of *which* has shifted to the woman herself. The sentence is concluded with a present participle clause. The meaning is carried forward by *So*, which begins the next sentence – an example of the type just mentioned – and introduces a simile:

> So from *Lahai-roi's* Well some spicie cloud
> Woo'd by the Sun swels up to be his shrowd,
> And from his moist wombe weeps a fragrant showre,
> Which, scatter'd in a thousand pearls, each flowre
> And herb partakes, where having stood awhile
> And something coold the parch'd, and thirstie Isle,
> The thankful Earth unlocks her self, and blends,
> A thousand odours, which (all mixt,) she sends
> Up in one cloud, and so returns the skies
> That dew they lent, a breathing sacrifice.
>
> (11.53–62)

The two co-ordinate clauses following *So* are succeeded by another non-restrictive relative clause, a method of extending a clause complex much favoured by Vaughan. The clause continues after an included past participle clause: *scatter'd*. Then follows another *where* clause, which is again vague in reference. In this passage *where* clauses are the most loosely linked. The subject of the conjoined participle clauses: *having stood ...* and *something coold ...*, must be the *fragrant showre* but, following the conjunction *where* this is not immediately clear. Another non-restrictive relative clause follows *odours*, and a final co-ordinate clause ends the lengthy verse paragraph. Although divided into three sentences, one ending in a semi-colon, the connectives serve to bind the paragraph into one semantic whole. Counter-balancing this is the loose syntax of the two *where* clauses and the uncertain reference of the participle clauses. These weaken the structure and obscure the meaning.

This same piece may be used to examine the structure within the clauses. Apart from included participle clauses and prepositional adjuncts following the subject, the order here is invariably straightforward S V C and this, too, is typical of Vaughan. He has an occasional inversion but usually retains normal word order. In spite of the attempt to bind the verse paragraph into a coherent whole, the meaning, by the end, seems to have moved very far from Isaac. However, the next paragraph draws him back into the foreground with the line:

> Thus soar'd *thy* soul ...
> (1.63) [my italics]

Again we have the use of *thus* meaning 'in this way', which reminds the reader that the lengthy intervening passage is a simile. Here the connective both makes a parallel with what has gone before and links the new paragraph back to the first few lines of the preceding one. It is worth stressing the loose syntax of Vaughan's verse because it matches the theme of man's unrest and rejection of his Creator.

Man's restless state, which breaks the pattern of the 'sympathy' in Creation, is also reflected in the rhythms of Vaughan's verse. In the non-stanzaic poems in particular the semantic unit rarely coincides with the verse line. Frequent run-on lines and statements that finish in mid-line counterpoint the rhythm and, with their differing lengths, mirror the constant changes of mood described in the poems. The diverse lengths of line also contribute to the abrupt, rather jerky movement. The opening lines of 'Distraction' illustrate this:

> O knit me, that am crumbled dust! the heape
>   Is all dispers'd, and cheape;
>   Give for a handfull, but a thought
>   And it is bought;
> ...
>   The world
> Is full of voices; Man is call'd, and hurl'd
>   By each, he answers all,
>   Knows ev'ry note, and call.
>   (ll.1–4; 11–14)

The line lengths vary from five feet to one foot. They become progressively shorter at the beginning but they are irregularly placed through the poem. The longer lines are broken not only by the caesura but also by other pauses, and in the passage quoted above no syntactic unit is longer than six syllables; most are shorter. Lines frequently run on or end with a brief two or three-syllable unit, as in *and cheape*. The initial affricate of *cheap* also has a choppy effect and the voiceless consonants at the end of the rhyming words in the first four lines actually shorten the long vowels slightly.

Vaughan uses these rhythms in other ways, too, as at the end of this same poem. The movement of lines near the close has a dramatic effect, as the speaker addresses God in a miniature dramatic monologue:

> But now since thou didst blesse
> So much,
> I grieve, my God! that thou hast made me such.
> I grieve?
> O, yes! thou know'st I doe.
>
> (11.24–8)

The change of mood begins with the longer statement in the first two lines and those that follow become more leisurely because semantic and syntactic units are contained within the lines. Even the brief two-syllable question is less abrupt than the earlier short lines. The long vowel of the focal word *grieve* and the rising intonation of the question have the effect of lengthening the line. It lingers on the ear in a way that the previous short lines do not: they rush straight on to the line following, while the rhyme signals that a line-end has been reached. Here, after the question and answer, both made by the speaker, there follows a string of verbs of exhortation, all joined by the conjunction *and*. The repeated conjunctions also slacken the pace and the final verb is extended into a clause – long for this poem – of a line and a half. The final four lines, in effect, make up one clause, with the subject placed between two participle clauses, one past and one present, which could be analysed as modifiers:

> Come, and releive
> And tame, and keepe downe with thy light
> Dust that would rise, and dimme my sight,
> Lest left alone too long
> Amidst the noise, and throng,
> Opressd I
> Striving to save the whole, by parcells dye.
>
> (11.28–34)

The present participle clause at the beginning of the last line saves the main clause: *I ... by parcells dye*, from what would, without the interpolation, be an abrupt ending. Instead the clause ends on a falling cadence, which contrasts with the forceful imperative mood of the opening.

Drama, which is an essential part of Vaughan's overall structure in the sequence of the poems, is frequently enhanced by the syntax and rhythms of the verse. Like most metaphysical poets, he often conveys the idea of conversation through a leisurely rhythm. This tone is heard in 'I walkt the other day', especially in the initial clauses, which give the impression of engaging the reader in casual conversation. Another example, achieved partly through an apparent address to the reader, is the opening of 'The Palm-tree':

> Deare friend sit down, and bear awhile this shade
> As I have yours long since.
>
> (11.1–2)

The first four words are taken straight from Herbert's 'Love Unknown' and it emerges in Vaughan's poem that the soul is addressing the body. The conversational tone is continued through the first three stanzas by lengthy clause complexes, which run across stanzas and are in normal prose order.[12]

At other times, Vaughan's poems begin dramatically and abruptly in an exclamatory way, as 'Begging' (II):

> I, [Aye] do not go! thou know'st, I'le dye!
>
> (1.1)

Such dramatic verse is not confined to openings of poems. In the middle of 'The Proffer' we read:

> No, no; I am not he,
> Go seek elsewhere.
>
> (ll.31–2)

Like Herbert, Vaughan sometimes starts a poem *in medias res*, as 'The Stone':

> I have it now:
> But where to act, that none shall know,
> Where I shall have no cause to fear
>   An eye or ear,
> What man will show?
>
> (ll.1–5)

However, some caution is needed. Although still dramatic, the beginning of 'And do they so?' is not so strange as the deictic pronoun *they* without an obvious anaphoric reference may suggest:

> And do they so? have they a Sense
> Of ought but Influence?
>
> (ll.1–2)

The pronoun refers directly to the Latin quotation from Romans at the head of the poem:

> *Etenim res Creatae exerto Capite observantes expectant revelationem Filiorum Dei.* [For the earnest expectation of the creature waiteth for the manifestation of the sons of God.]
>
> (Romans,VIII.19)

This is often the case. If the titles and epigraphs are not read as integral parts of the poems, the meaning is often unclear. Unlike Herbert, Vaughan rarely addresses God directly. He frequently apostrophizes the deity but the effect is less abrupt than that of many of Herbert's poems. Compare the beginning of Vaughan's 'The Resolve':

> I have consider'd it; and find
>   A longer stay
> Is but excus'd neglect;
>
> (ll.1–3)

with Herbert's 'The Reprisall':

> I have consider'd it, and finde
> There is no dealing with thy mighty passion.
> (11.1–2)

Vaughan's first line is a word for word borrowing from Herbert but he not only shifts the structure away from that of direct address but also, by breaking up the lines and, hence, the rhythm, he introduces again the more leisurely pace of thoughtful conversation. The clause following *find* is the same metrical length in both poets. Vaughan's line arrangement, however, enforces a pause after *stay*, which slows the pace and removes the impetus of the headlong rush which marks Herbert's emphatic statement. Like Herbert, Vaughan frequently uses such sentence fillers as *sure* which contribute to the notion of a speech-based verse. In actual representation of speech, Vaughan also uses colloquial expressions, as in 'The Ornament':

> While one cryed out, We are disgrac'd
> For she is bravest, you confess.
> (11.19–20)

The comment clause *you confess* is also a type of speech filler, giving the impression of verisimilitude to a short speech.

In contrast to this loose, colloquial form of expression, Vaughan frequently includes very tight-knit, elliptical phrases and clauses. Ellipsis is a feature of most of the metaphysical poets. In 'The Storm' the last line of the following quotation is such a clause:

> Dark storms, and wind
> Incite them to that fierce discusse,
> Else not Inclin'd.
> (11.10–12)

Occasionally these compressed expressions are placed in parentheses, as in 'Vanity of Spirit':

> I tooke them up, and (much Joy'd,) went about ...
> (1.25)

and in 'Buriall':

> The world's thy boxe: how then (there tost,)
>   Can I be lost?
>
> (11.31–2)

The second example has both a compressed and conversational effect in spite of the stylization of the ellipsis. It is rather like an aside in speech. Most of the many parenthetical phrases and clauses are of this type and add to the impression of a speaking voice. Similar is (*to spend my hour*) in 'I walkt the other day'. Here there is no ellipsis and the phrase reads like an afterthought, casually, almost inconsequentially, added.

Among other features of Vaughan's language are his liking for proverbs and proverbial-type sayings, often deriving ultimately from the biblical Proverbs, and the slight but not insignificant use of vocabulary drawn from worldly affairs, including war. This last shows that Vaughan was not unaffected by the turbulent times in which he lived – indeed, they were the reason for his withdrawal from public life.

Sufficient features of Vaughan's language have been touched on to show his great diversity. He is less easy to talk about in overall terms than other metaphysical poets, including Herbert, from whom he borrowed so extensively and who was one of his chief sources of inspiration. To contain Vaughan's poetry is like trying to hold water in a sieve. Neither meaning nor language will submit to a compact all-inclusive survey.

6 Thomas Traherne (1637–74)

> *'not the Objects, but the Sence*
> *Of Things'*
> ('Desire')

Unlike most of the other metaphysical poets Traherne wrote no secular poetry. His subject matter is wholly religious and basically he has one main theme: man has been created to enjoy the world, which, like himself, has been made by God. His enjoyment and gratitude to his Maker make him a partaker in God's divinity and complete God's joy in his Creation:

> ... all the business of Religion on GODS part is Bounty, Gratitude on ours, and ... this Gratitude is the sphere of all Vertue and Felicity.
>
> (*CE*, 284)[1]

Without this cyclical movement the purpose of Creation remains unfulfilled. The immediate theory comes straight from the Cambridge Platonists, with whose writing Traherne was familiar.[2] It is not unlike Vaughan's hermeticism. In many ways Traherne's thinking is akin to Vaughan's. In Traherne's poetry, however, the 'busy commerce kept between/ God and his creatures' is restricted to man and God. The other parts of Creation are the means by which man apprehends the deity. The theme is reflected in various ways in Traherne's language, particularly in vocabulary. It also makes for paradox. In the beginning Man is ignorant of evil. But as the soul becomes infused with the spirit of God, it sees things from the viewpoint of eternity and can even rejoice in evil as a part of God's total Creation:

> Even Trades them selvs seen in Celestial Light
> And Cares and Sins and Woes are Bright.
> ('The Vision' 11.7–8)

It might seem that a single theme would make for repetition. Traherne put his poems in a sequence, however, so that one poem grows out of another. The progress of the soul is thereby traced. Man starts as an infant, 'newly clothd with Skin' ('The Preparative', 1.10), but at the end of the sequence he is mature in that he has overcome the boundaries of time and space, and achieved the vision of eternity which enfolds everything in delight:

> God is the Object, and God is the Way of Enjoying. God in all his Excellencies, Laws and Works, in all his Ways and Counsels is the Soveraign Object of all Felicitie. Eternity and Time, Heaven and Earth, Kingdoms and Ages, Angels and Men, are in him to be enjoyed.
> (The Fifth Century, I, 226)[3]

As a result of this schematic subject matter Traherne uses more abstract language than any other metaphysical poet. He is similar to Donne in that the words he uses are no guide to the content of his poems. To list words would not give the reader much idea of the theme of the poetry. The areas from which he draws his vocabulary are restricted, as are the words themselves. In this he differs from the other metaphysical poets. Many of the same words appear time after time. It is the way in which Traherne uses them that is important.

The first poem in the sequence is 'The Salutation':

> 1
> These little Limmes,
> These Eys and Hands, which here I find,
> These rosie Cheeks wherwith my Life begins,
> Where have ye been? Behind

5   What Curtain were ye from me hid so long!
       Where was? in what Abyss, my Speaking Tongue?

2
When silent I,
So many thousand thousand yeers,
Beneath the Dust did in a Chaos lie,
10   How could I Smiles or Tears,
Or Lips or Hands or Eys or Ears perceiv?
Welcom ye Treasures which I now receiv.

3
I that so long
Was Nothing from Eternitie,
15   Did little think such Joys as Ear or Tongue,
To Celebrat or See:
Such Sounds to hear, such Hands to feel, such Feet,
Beneath the Skies, on such a Ground to meet.

4
New Burnisht Joys!
20   Which yellow Gold and Pearl excell!
Such Sacred Treasures are the Lims in Boys,
In which a Soul doth Dwell;
Their Organized Joynts, and Azure Veins
More Wealth include, then all the World contains.

5
25   From Dust I rise,
And out of Nothing now awake,
These Brighter Regions which salute mine Eys,
A Gift from GOD I take.
The Earth, the Seas, the Light, the Day, the Skies,
30   The Sun and Stars are mine; if those I prize.

6
Long time before
I in my Mothers Womb was born,
A GOD preparing did this Glorious Store,
The World for me adorne.

35 Into this Eden so Divine and fair,
    So Wide and Bright, I com his Son and Heir.

                              7
            A Stranger here
        Strange Things doth meet, Strange Glories See;
        Strange Treasures lodg'd in this fair World appear,
40   Strange all, and New to me.
        But that they mine should be, who nothing was,
        That Strangest is of all, yet brought to pass.

Abstract words abound. The first concrete nouns denote parts of the body: *Limmes*; *Eys*; *Hands*; *Cheeks* and *Tongue*. Later we have *Lips*; *Ears* and *Feet*. These recur throughout Traherne's verse. They are important to his philosophy. They are the means through which man first apprehends God's Creation. There is little sense of the particular, however. In 'Their Organized Joynts, and Azure Veins' (1.23) the adjective *Azure*, collocating with *Veins*, conjures up a more visual image than is usual but it remains general since it refers back to 'Lims in Boys' (1.21), which are themselves unspecified. When Traherne uses adjectives they are mostly of the type in *Organized Joynts*, which presents a structural concept.

Another set of concrete words has to do with the various parts of the physical world: 'The Earth, the Seas, the Light, the Day, the Skies,/ The Sun and Stars ...' (11.29–30). It might be said that *Light* and *Day* are not truly concrete. They are, however, palpable and always associated in Traherne's poetry with properties of the physical world. Traherne's vocabulary falls into categories that do not necessarily correspond with conventional groupings of any kind, semantic or otherwise.

The last group of concrete words in this poem is part of a semantic group denoting precious stones and metals: *yellow Gold and Pearl* (1.20). These words appear in large numbers throughout Traherne's verse and, initially, because they occur in poetry that has a religious theme, put the reader in mind of the book of Revelation in the Bible. However, as used by Traherne, they usually represent 'negative' values. Although part of the natural, physical world, they belong to the dark side of Creation. The *Limmes*, with which they are compared in this poem, 'excell' them.

The half-concrete half-abstract words mentioned earlier raise a crucial obstacle to understanding Traherne's language: where can the line be drawn between concrete and abstract language? *Chaos*; *World*; *Eternitie*; *Joys*; *Treasures* and *Glories* seem to be typical of the abstract nouns that he uses. However, although they would normally be classified in one broad band of abstract words, in Traherne's usage they fall into different categories. Such words as *Treasures*; *Glories* and even *Joys* (note the plural, which has a slightly different meaning from *Joy*) are partly concrete, since they, or at least their physical manifestations, can be apprehended through the senses. They tend towards the abstract, however, and are always used in a general way. These 'half-way' words attract Traherne and make up a large part of his abstract vocabulary. The three words just given occur repeatedly. Even in this one poem *Treasures* and *World*, which is another word that falls into the same set, occur three times each and, although there is only one instance of *Glories*, there is also one of the derivative *Glorious*.

Traherne's biblical language is also important. The co-ordinated nouns *Son and Heir*, associated with *Eden*, take on a clear biblical significance. Much of Traherne's language is of this sort, although direct references to the Bible and to biblical characters are relatively few.

Adjectives have already received comment. Premodifying adjectives are fewer than predicative ones and most, except for the colour adjectives *rosie*, *yellow* and *Azure*, are non-visual and abstract. Like the nouns, they often come in strings:

> ... this Eden so Divine and fair,
> So Wide and Bright ...
>
> (11.35–6)

These lines include another feature of Traherne's language: the intensifier *so*. He uses intensifiers frequently. In the third stanza of this poem *such* occurs before the noun *Sounds*. This is the equivalent of *so* before adjectives. The prevalence of intensifiers, used loosely as here, is one reason why Traherne's poetry has sometimes been criticized as mere wordy effusion that lacks strenuous thought.

Traherne's use of verbs is not unlike that of other metaphysical poets. In this poem there are relatively few finite verbs: thirty-one, roughly two in every three lines of verse. Of these, nine are parts of the verb *be*. Stanza 3 has only two finite verbs, the cognitive *did think* and *Was*. Only *rise*; *awake*; *salute*; *take*; *adorne*; *com*; *brought to pass* and possibly *to Celebrat* could be said to be in any sense actively dynamic. The rest are stative (cognitive or verbs of inert perception) or, like *receive*, have passive connotations. Traherne uses strongly dynamic verbs sparingly.

Typically, there is no metaphor in this poem. Unlike other metaphysical poets, Traherne rarely uses it. Neither is there much use of any other of the more common figures of speech, such as simile or even hyperbole. Yet in one sense the language is always 'excessive' and, partly because of the use of intensifiers, the impression conveyed by this poem, as by most others, is hyperbolic. One clear rhetorical device that Traherne uses is repetition. In this poem the first type of repetition to strike the reader is repetition of words, particularly in the final stanza where the word *strange*, or derivatives of it, occurs six times. Repetition of words and sentence structures contributes to the sense of hyperbole but also has a further part to play in this poem. The reiteration of *stranger* emphasizes that at the beginning of his conscious life man does not know the world into which he has been born. Key words are often stressed by this means. Likewise, syntactic frames are repeated, as in the third stanza:

> Such Sounds to hear, such Hands to feel, such Feet,
> Beneath the Skies, on such a Ground to meet.
>
> (11.17–18)

The repetition, skilfully varied, draws the reader's attention to the multitude of wonders, often those we take for granted, in the world about us. The repeated intensifier *such* also forwards meaning – it is not a space-filler. In subsequent poems, which unfold God's purpose and man's place in the scheme of things, repetition does not always have this particular function.

Traherne's exclamatory sentences also contribute to the inherent meaning. So do the many questions, which come only at the beginning of the poem. Questions are not usual. Traherne's preference is for statement or exclamation. In this poem the initial questions convey the sense of wonder and surprise at the infant's discovery of its own physical nature. Apart from exclamations, Traherne's sentence structure is generally straightforward and right-branching, the clauses following normal S V C prose order. In this poem there are rather more inversions of clauses and parts of clauses than in Traherne's poetry as a whole.

The linguistic features of this first poem are typical of Traherne's poetry generally. Nouns naming outward parts of the body are plentiful. There are also words that denote internal parts. Some of these occur in 'The Person':

> when we see
> The Anatomie,
> Survey the Skin, cut up the Flesh, the Veins
> Unfold: The Glory there remains.
> The Muscles, Fibres, Arteries and Bones ...
> (11.27–31)

The naming of inner physical organs demonstrates Traherne's belief that we realize the wonder of things only by seeing into their essence. The poet says his purpose is not

> to bring
> New Robes, but to Display the Thing:
> Nor Paint, Nor Cloath, Nor Crown, nor add a Ray,
> But Glorify by taking all away.
> (11.13–16)

Natural objects should not be decked out in fancy – or poetical – dress which hides their inner truth. This is the reason for Traherne's almost complete rejection of metaphor, although in 'The Person' and other poems he does have recourse to brief metaphorical expressions.

There are relatively few concrete nouns denoting natural objects in the poems. A few come into 'The Demonstration':

> And Nothing's truly seen that's Mean:
> Be it a Sand, an Acorn, or a Bean,
> It must be clothd with Endless Glory.
> (11.25–7)

Here, as often, physical objects are named but not dwelt on or described. Traherne stresses the fact that even the most trivial natural objects are 'clothd with Endless Glory' in the sight of God and also in that of man once he has attained God's perspective. Man-made things, on the other hand, represent empty and worthless values. This is not the way in which Herbert, say, uses objects taken from urban and domestic life. One example from 'Eden' is:

> Vain Costly Toys,
> Swearing and Roaring Boys,
> Shops, Markets, Taverns, Coaches ...
> (11.23–5)

Traherne's attitude is immediately clear from the adjective *Vain*. The poem continues to say that in infancy these features (some human) of town life were *then unknown*. The temporal adverb *then* refers back ultimately to the last line of the preceding poem 'Wonder': 'When I was born'. *Then* is the first indication of 'time' in this poem. The way it follows on the end of the previous poem, 'Wonder', shows how the poems are linked together in sequence. The first line of 'Eden' reads:

> A learned and a Happy Ignorance
> Divided me,
> From all the Vanitie ...
> ... Sloth Care Pain and Sorrow ...
> (11.1–4)

Although man-made objects and things appertaining to civilized living usually have negative connotations, Traherne's attitude is not always consistent. In 'Wonder' he speaks of them as *Cursd and Devisd Proprieties* and names the various restrictive things in man's world: *Hedges, Ditches, Limits, Bounds*. It is clear that these words of demarcation fall into the same semantic 'set', or an overlapping one, as the other words denoting man-made objects. In the following stanza he lists other things which also enclose space: *Walls, Boxes, Coffers*. In this case the infant is either unaware of them: 'I dreamt not ought of those', or accepts them as part of his domain:

> Proprieties themselvs were mine,
> And Hedges Ornaments.
> (11.57–8)

The *Boxes* and *Coffers* 'Did not Divide my Joys, but all combine'. The word *proprieties*, related to *property*, which implies ownership, embodies a pun. In using this word, Traherne 'appropriates' to the child things which contain or mark off the 'property' of individuals. When man is fully aware of the world in Traherne's sense, everything becomes again the 'property' of each.

Immediately after this comes another list relating to dress:

> Clothes, Ribbans, Jewels, Laces, I esteemd
>   My Joys by others worn.
>   (11.61–2)

These articles of dress and ornament are also in some way confining. Note the use of *Manicles* in collocation with similar ornaments in 'The Person':

> ... Golden Chains and Bracelets are
> But Gilded Manicles, wherby
>   Old Satan doth ensnare,
>   Allure, Bewitch the Ey.
>   (11.55–8)

The link with the other limiting objects is not, therefore, excluded.

A slightly different use is made of material objects in 'The Estate'. Speaking once more of the physical parts of the body, Traherne says:

> They ought, my God, to be the Pipes,
>   And Conduits of thy Prais.
>   (11.29–30)

This is nearer to Herbert's use of this kind of vocabulary. In Traherne it embodies his central theme: the continual interaction between God and man, in which God gives and man completes the gift by returning thanks and gratitude. But this usage is not typical. It comes in one of Traherne's rare metaphors, which may be why it seems nearer to Herbert.

Another group of concrete nouns noted in the first poem names precious stones and metals. These, too, are many and, although part of the natural world, nearly always have a negative connotation. An example occurs in 'The Recovery':

> All Gold and Silver is but Empty Dross
> Rubies and Saphires are but Loss.
> (11.64–5)

Traherne does use this type of word in a 'positive' sense, but only rarely. The following lines come in 'Wonder':

> Rich Diamond and Pearl and Gold
> In evry Place was seen;
> ...
> That and my Wealth was evry where:
> No Joy to this!
> (11.41–2; 47–8)

These lines come at the very beginning of the sequence, before the infant soul is aware of evil things. It accepts and appropriates to itself everything within its field of vision.

Conversely, a 'negative' attitude to words denoting objects in the physical world, occurs in 'Desire':

> Where are the Silent Streams,
> The Living Waters, and the Glorious Beams,
> The Sweet Reviving Bowers,
> The Shady Groves, the Sweet and Curious Flowers,
> The Springs and Trees, The Heavenly Days,
> The Flowry Meads, the Glorious Rayes,
> The Gold and Silver Towers?
> (11.27–33)

This language foreshadows that of early eighteenth-century poetry. It sounds distinctly 'artificial' and this is reinforced by the collocation with *Gold* and *Silver*. The customary 'negative' meaning of these adjectives is clear as they premodify *Towers*, which are man-made buildings. The poem continues with a list of the same natural objects repeated, largely without modification:

> Alass, all these are poor and Empty Things,
>   Trees Waters Days and Shining Beams
> Fruits, Flowers, Bowers, Shady Groves and Springs,
> No Joy will yeeld, no more then Silent Streams.
>   These are but Dead Material Toys,
>   And cannot make my Heavenly Joys.
>   (11.34–9)

Natural objects are now rejected. This is not a confusion in Traherne's thinking or in the way he manipulates his vocabulary, but a deliberate use to demonstrate man's spiritual progress. This poem comes towards the end of the sequence when the soul has so far advanced that it no longer needs the support of objects apprehended by the physical senses; it is ready to partake directly of the joy of heavenly things as God, its Creator, does:

> Whatever Pleasures are at his right Hand
>   Ye must, before I am Divine,
>   In full Proprietie be mine.
>   (11.50–2)

Again there is the semantic link between *Proprietie* and 'property'. On another occasion Traherne seems to confuse the value he normally puts on certain words. In 'The Estate' gold and silver are associated with natural objects such as the sun:

> The Sun it self doth in its Glory Shine,
> And Gold and Silver out of very Mire,
> And Pearls and Rubies out of Earth refine,
>   While Herbs and Flowers aspire
>   To touch and make our feet Divine.
>   (11.63–7)

Philip Traherne, the poet's brother, who prepared a selection of the poems for publication, obviously thought that the usage was not consistent with Thomas's intentions. He changed these lines in the manuscript and eliminated *Gold and Silver* and *Pearls and Rubies*:

> The Orb of Light in its wide Circuit movs,
> Corn for our Food Springs out of very Mire,

Fences and Fewel grow in Woods and Groves.[4]

It is possible that Philip was mistaken. This poem is near the end of the sequence. Thomas Traherne's mixing of these sets of words may be intended to indicate that man has almost come full circle in his progress back to God. When he began the pilgrimage at the beginning of the sequence, he was able to accept all things through ignorance; now he is approaching the stage where he can accept through knowlege and understanding. He has almost attained the perspective of his Maker. Thus, certain 'sets' of words have shifting meanings. Traherne uses them as if they were counters, representing values that change during the course of the cycle of poems. It is clear that Traherne's use of even apparently straightforward words is far from simple.

There were some biblical allusions in 'The Salutation', although, as remarked, Traherne's direct references to the Bible are few. They come mostly from the Old Testament: Adam, Eden and the Serpent are named, as are Elijah, Elisha and David. There is very little elaboration or use of the events recorded of these characters. There is emblematic reference to objects associated with them: Elijah's chariot, Elisha's blindness and David's Temple; their significance is not explained; they are simply stated. Strikingly, Traherne names Christ only once, in 'Thoughts. IV.', the penultimate poem in the sequence. In the same poem there is one of two references to the New Jerusalem and also to Elijah and Elisha. In spite of the relatively few biblical characters and specific events mentioned, Traherne's language is based on the Bible and the tradition of Christian meditation. Occasionally there is a direct, or nearly direct, quotation, as in *the Apple of my Eye* ('My Spirit', 1.62). This comes in the Psalms (XVII.8) and elsewhere and is quoted in the Office of Compline. Constant references to *Living Streams*; *Living Water*; *Bride*; *Bridegroom* and similar words and phrases show how readily biblical language came to Traherne. Usually he slips in such references so unobtrusively that the reader may not be aware of them. Examples are *Talents* ('The Circulation', 1.56); *Tabernacle* and *Palmes* ('The Enquirie', 11.17; 18). One poem that seems to draw directly on biblical images is 'Dumnesse':

My foes puld down the Temple to the ground,
...
    they march out thence
In Troops that Cover and despoyl my Coasts,
Being the Invisible, most Hurtfull Hosts.
                                    (11.71; 76–8)

Temple and *Hosts*, as well as the war-like activity, bring passages of the Old Testament to mind. Other nouns, such as *Myrrh*; *Aloes*; *Incense* and so on are constantly used. In addition there are references to church furniture, such as *Pulpit* and *Organ*; the word *Priest* also occurs. Generally the language of the Bible underpins Traherne's usage.

Classical allusions, found in Donne and Crashaw, are also rare but they do occur in one poem, 'Love':

And Jove beyond the Fiction doth appear
    Once more in Golden Rain to come
    To Danae's Pleasing Fruitfull Womb.
                                    (11.28–30)

Traherne is indicating the way in which Joys are showered from heaven on man, who is Jove's *Ganimede*:

    His Ganimede! His life! His joy!
Or he comes down to me, or takes me up
        That I might be his Boy,
And fill, and taste, and give, and Drink the Cup ...
                                    (11.31–4)

Man is more than Ganimede for he is not only the cup-bearer but shares the cup with his Lord. This, apart from another isolated use of *Jove*, is the total extent of Traherne's use of classical mythology and even here he places it at a remove from myth by the striking phrase *beyond the Fiction*.

In many poems Traherne uses more clearly abstract nouns than he does in the poem examined at the beginning of the chapter. Abstract qualities are *Truth*; *Innocence*; *Delight* and *Felicity*. *Beauty* is another such word but in Traherne's vocabulary it has connotations of the concrete, as does *Glories*. Traherne also uses abstract words for virtues and vices, moods and emotions: *Penitence*; *Avarice*; *Wantonness*; *Woes*; *Delight*; *Sorrow*; *Gratitude*; and also for such feelings as *Thirst and Hunger*, used in a non-physical sense. Other abstract words are those like *Means*; *End*; *Cause*; *Influence*; *Intelligence*; *Conceptions* and *Thoughts*, which is the title of four poems. Words of this kind convey the more intellectual concepts through which the reader is intended to see into the significance of the material objects round him:

> Thoughts are the Things
> That us affect: The Hony and the Stings
> Of all that is, are Seated in a Thought,
> Even while it seemeth weak, and next to Nought.
> (' Thoughts. III.' 11.21–4)

Here is one of Traherne's rare metaphors, typically short and unelaborated. It is a repetition of one that he uses earlier in the sequence in 'The Preparative'. As an infant, he says:

> I did receiv
> The fair Ideas of all Things,
> And had the Hony even without the Stings.
> (11.24–6)

The intellectual nature of the nouns just cited is an integral part of Traherne's thinking and an aspect of his writing which has often been overlooked. They could be said to be the most essentially abstract of the words that he uses. Alongside abstract nouns are correspondingly abstract adjectives, such as *Meditating* and *Inward* from the stanza of 'The Preparative' quoted above.

Traherne's use of verbs has affinities with his use of abstract nouns and adjectives. At times nouns, particularly abstract ones, and verbs can scarcely be separated. Verbs, as noted earlier, are mainly stative. Some more dynamic ones occur in 'Dumnesse': *hoop, Cry, roar, Call*, but these are explicitly associated with *mine Enemies*, just as the rather similar 'Swearing and Roaring Boys' of 'Eden' (1.24) are part of a world blind to God's purpose. Since the initial vital forces in the poems come through the senses, it is not surprising that Traherne uses verbs of inert perception, either in nominal or verbal form. Man 'sees, and feels, and Smels, and Lives' ('The Demonstration', 1.71). The words *taste*; *hear*; *thirst* and *hunger* also occur. Later the growing soul is able to apprehend through its intelligence or intellect. This progression is marked largely, although not always, through stative, often cognitive, verbs. In 'The Anticipation', which comes over half way through the sequence, man has passed beyond the world about him to grasp the nature of its Maker. The poem focuses on God and his attributes:

> His Essence is all Act: He did, that He
>   All Act might always be.
> His Nature burns like fire;
> His Goodness infinitly doth desire,
>   To be by all possest;
> It is the Glory of his High Estate,
> And that which I for ever more Admire,
> He is an Act that doth Communicate.
>   (11.91-9)

Did in the first line and *be* in the second are lexically full verbs, not auxiliaries. We saw earlier that Donne often uses such verbs, especially *be*. Unlike *do*, *be* is a stative verb, but as it is used here it assumes dynamic force. The lines are dominated by the noun *Act*, which takes on the nature of a dynamic verb through the meaning it conveys and by collocation with *did*. This is one instance where a noun is virtually inseparable from a verb. Traherne has other ways in which he expresses the movements of the intellect. In 'My Spirit' the outward movement of the expanding soul is conveyed through the simple phrase *but evry Where*:

> In its own Centre is a Sphere
> Not shut up here, but evry Where.
>   (11.16-17)

Two points stand out: stative verbs often assume the semantic function of dynamic verbs and secondly, whereas large numbers of nouns usually result in static language, in Traherne's verse they emphasize energy and activity. The *Act* of God *communicates*. Another example comes in the poem 'The Circulation':

> All Things to Circulations owe
> Themselvs; by which alone
> They do exist.
>
> (11.29–31)

The abstract and Latinate noun *Circulations* seems an unlikely candidate for verbal significance but in context it indicates the movement at the very heart of the sequence: the cyclical outpouring of God's bounty and man's return of praise and thanksgiving that completes Creation. These nouns embody action that is normally carried by verbs. Although Traherne's verbs are rarely dynamic in a technical sense and his language overall is essentially noun-based, the effect is not what might be expected from noun-based writing.

Repetition in Traherne's verse has already been noted. Repetition of individual words is frequent. These are usually nouns but grammatical words are also repeated. An example involving pronouns is the following from 'Another':

> He seeks for ours as we do seek for his.
> Nay O my Soul, ours is far more His Bliss
> Then his is ours.
>
> (11.1–3)

This type of repetition recalls Donne, although it has neither the riddling quality of the earlier poet nor is it a constant feature of Traherne's language. Again it is necessary to turn to the last lines of the previous poem, 'The Recovery', to discover the meaning of the crucial pronouns *his* and *ours*:

> One Voluntary Act of Love
> Far more Delightfull to his Soul doth prove.
>
> (11.68–9)

Traherne uses many different sentence types and structures. Examples of exclamations and questions came in 'The Salutation' (pp.128–30). Apostrophe is also frequent. His straightforward statements vary in length from one short clause to those which occupy a whole stanza of six or more lines and contain co-ordinate and different types of subordinate clauses.

'The Anticipation' has a variety of clause types. One stanza with a series of short statements is:

> The End in Him from Everlasting is
>   The Fountain of all Bliss.
> From Everlasting it
> Efficient was, and Influence did Emit,
>   That caused all. Before
>   The World, we do Adore
> This Glorious End. Becaus all Benefit
> From it proceeds. Both are the very same.
> The End and Fountain differ but in Name.
>   (11.28–36)

There are five punctuated sentences, all except the second of only one clause. The full stop after *Glorious End* in the seventh line marks a pause before the following dependent *because* clause. This is the reason for 'adoration'. The stop also marks the contrast between *Before*, with which the statement begins, and *End*. The following stanza has a much more complex structure:

> That so the End should be the very Spring,
>   Of evry Glorious Thing;
>   And that which seemeth Last,
> The Fountain and the Caus; attaind so fast,
>   That it was first; and movd
>   The Efficient, who so lovd
> All Worlds and made them for the sake of this
> It shews the End Compleat before, and is
> A Perfect Token of his Perfect Bliss.
>   (11.37–45)

That so in the first line means 'so that' or 'in order that' (Herbert uses the same word order in 'Deniall' and 'The Watercourse') and picks up the proposition of the previous stanza: that the End and Beginning are one and the same, a concept familiar from all traditional Christian meditation. It is Traherne's main theme. The third line and first half of the fourth line constitute a clause co-ordinate with the first two and parallel in meaning. By its position *Caus* would seem to be the antecedent of the following past participle clause, *attaind so fast*, but semantically the clause refers back to *End*. It is not easy to grasp the connection on first reading since the past participle *attaind* is so far removed from its antecedent. Traherne intends to demonstrate that the *End* is also *The Fountain* or 'beginning' and it does not in fact matter whether the clause is attached to *End* or *Caus*. The past participle clause and its first subordinate clause of result state the proposition once again. The co-ordinate clause of result: *and movd/ The Efficient*, that is the 'thing which *effected*', in other words *the Caus*, has two co-ordinate relative clauses attached. The word *so* before *lovd* is one of Traherne's rare intensifiers that are used loosely. It is an echo of John III.16: 'God so loved the world'. The stanza concludes with two more co-ordinate clauses, completing the pattern of co-ordination. The first restates the initial proposition and the second goes back to an idea expressed earlier in the poem:

> From Everlasting His felicitie
> Compleat and perfect was.
> (11.22–3)

These clauses have been taken as independent main clauses but if the lack of punctuation after *this* (1.43) is intentional, they could be adverbial clauses of result. Traherne's syntax is not always so complicated, even when he uses long clause complexes. The overall meaning of this particular poem is clear in spite of the syntactical difficulties. The central paradox is restated throughout the poem.

Traherne often uses exclamatory sentences. They tend to occur in clusters and sometimes one will run over several lines. 'The Rapture' is made up almost entirely of short exclamations in short lines. The first two stanzas read:

> Sweet Infancy!
> O fire of Heaven! O Sacred Light!
> How Fair and Bright!
> How Great am I,
> Whom all the World doth magnifie!

> O Heavenly Joy!
> O Great and Sacred Blessedness,
>   Which I possess!
>   So great a Joy
> Who did into my Armes convey!
>   (ll.1–10)

This type of writing is quite different from that of 'The Anticipation' and brings to mind Blake's 'Infant Joy' and other 'Songs of Innocence'. Indeed, Traherne's vision of the unity of Creation has much in common with Blake's.

In 'The Rapture' the penultimate line, which runs on to the last, results in awkward phrasing because of the metrical pattern. Traherne usually contrives to maintain normal prose order. The first stanza quoted from 'The Anticipation' has no less than five run-on lines and three statements end in mid line, without sacrificing either the metre or the normal syntactical order. This is a regular feature and it is easy to overlook the skill with which it is handled. Although the metre is sometimes strained it seldom breaks down. On the other hand, this sort of writing lacks the qualities of more lyrical poetry. The insistence on the theme can make it seem 'flat' in a way that Herbert's verse, which also has a certain prosaic quality, never is. Traherne occasionally achieves poetic heights in isolated passages and lines. These usually come in metaphor or other figures but are also sometimes effected through rhythm. The beginning of 'Speed' affords an example:

> The Liquid Pearl in Springs,
> The usefull and the Precious Things
> Are in a Moment Known.
>   (ll.1–3)

This recalls the cadences of Herbert. The metre is basically that of a three-foot iambic line but the second line has two extra syllables. The extended rhythm, together with the rhyme with the previous shorter line, introduces a variety that is often lacking in Traherne's measures. The lengthy nominal groups of the two appositive subjects are brought to a musically satisfying conclusion in the final line, which reverts to the standard length. This metrical pattern is not kept up in the following stanzas and one can easily hear the difference when all the lines are the same length:

I was as High and Great,
As Kings are in their Seat.
All other Things were mine.
(11.13–15)

The predictable nature of line lengths, especially of the two rhyming lines, and the end stopping do not have the same musical cadence. Sometimes run-on lines lift this kind of verse. Here is the opening of another stanza in this same poem:

New all! New Burnisht Joys;
Tho now by other Toys
Ecclypst: New all and mine.
(11.25–7)

Again unexpectedness infuses the lines with a certain excitement. Although the lines match metrically, the final statement is a foot shorter. In addition there is ellipsis of verb, inversion and repetition. So many features in such a short space raise the emotional level. However, metrical variations do not necessarily bring poetic quality. The third stanza of 'The Circulation' has variety both of line and sentence length but remains uncompromisingly prosaic in sound:

All Things to Circulations owe
    Themselvs; by which alone
They do exist.
(11.29–31)

There is perhaps too much variation here. The ear cannot catch an underlying rhythm from which the lines deviate. Explication, as so often in Traherne, becomes laboured because he has to seek hard to find words to convey a meaning which is either strange or elusive. Consequently, instead of ellipsis, we have an almost too wordy statement.

Occasional lyrical lines are probably fortuitous. Traherne could write lyrically as he proves in his prose. Indeed his prose is often more poetic than his verse. In the poetry he sacrifices all other considerations for the sake of his meaning. The constraints of the stanza forms, often intricate, force him into a type of expression that he could avoid in prose. These constraints account for some weak lines, especially those which rhyme or fall at the end of a stanza. There are several examples in 'The Salutation': *which I now receiv* (1.11) at the end of the second stanza; *if those I prize* (1.30) at the end of the fifth; and the final clause *yet brought to pass* (1.42). All of these are tags to fill up the line. The clause at the end of stanza six, however, is semantically full and has a fine cadence:

> Into this Eden so Divine and fair,
> So Wide and Bright, I com his Son and Heir.
> (11.35–6)

Here the main part of the clause is deferred to the end. This and the coincidence of stress with lexically full words impart a jaunty rhythm that matches the movement of a springing step, even though the actual movement is spiritual rather than physical.

Repetition of individual words in Traherne's verse is frequent, as already noted. Repetition also involves parallel phrases and clauses. The last stanza of 'The Salutation', the poem examined at the beginning of this chapter, is a good example of variations of repeated clause structures. Often the frame is repeated more exactly, as in the following from 'The Recovery', which has three parallel clauses, the second slightly lengthened and the third extended not only by four parallel complements but by a final postmodifying relative clause:

> ... Gratitude, Thanksgiving, Prais,
> A Heart returnd for all these Joys,
> These are the Things admird,
> These are the Things by Him desird.
> These are the Nectar and the Quintessence
> The Cream and Flower that most affect his Sence.
> (11.55–60)

There is a longer example of repeated clause structures in 'Dumnesse', a poem full of such parallels:

> It was with Cleerer Eys
> To see all Creatures full of Deities;
> Especialy Ones self: And to Admire
> The Satisfaction of all True Desire:
> Twas to be Pleasd with all that God hath done;
> Twas to Enjoy *even All* beneath the Sun:
> Twas with a steddy and immediat Sence
> To feel and measure all the Excellence
> Of Things: Twas to inherit Endless Treasure,
> And to be fild with Everlasting Pleasure:
> To reign in Silence, and to Sing alone
> To see, love, Covet, hav, Enjoy and Prais, in one:
> To Prize and to be ravishd: to be true,
> Sincere and Single in a Blessed View
> Of all his gifts,
>
> (11.39–53)

This lengthy sequence of some twenty parallel clauses was cut to seven by Philip Traherne in his revision of the poem for publication. He also omits line 50, which consists almost entirely of the six infinitives. Perhaps he felt the parallelism had gone too far in this instance.

Compared with the other metaphysical poets Traherne makes little use of figurative language and imagery. He rejects metaphor as a general principle of perception. In 'The Person' he says:

> The Naked Things
> Are most Sublime, and Brightest shew,
> When they alone are seen:
> ...
> Their Worth they then do best reveal,
> When we all Metaphores remove,
> For Metaphores conceal,
> And only Vapours prove.
>
> (11.17–19; 23–6)

He carries the spirit of this principle into his writing generally, although he sometimes uses incidental and brief metaphors. Such metaphors usually consist of only one or two words. Just occasionally they are more overt as in 'Fullnesse', where he lists ways of describing *Bliss* in concrete terms:

> It is my Davids Tower,
> Where all my Armor lies,
> (11.21–2)

and:

> The Root of Hope, The Golden Chain,
> Whose End is, as the Poets feign,
>   Fastned to the very Throne
>   Of Jove.
>   It is a Stone
>   On which I sit.
> (11.28–33)[5]

Other apparently overt metaphors are almost certainly, as in the metaphors of Herbert and Crashaw, intended to be taken in a literal sense:

> Mens Sences are indeed the Gems,
>   Their Praises the most Sweet Perfumes,
> Their Eys the Thrones, their Hearts the Heavnly Rooms,
>   Their Souls the Diadems,
> Their Tongues the Organs ...
> ('The Enquirie' 11.19–23)

Two examples of simile occur in the last stanza of 'The Improvment':

> As Spunges gather Moisture from the Earth
> (Which seemeth Drie,) in which they buried are;
> As Air infecteth Salt; so at my Birth
> All these were unperceivd, yet did appear.
> (11.79–82)[6]

Similes are also used sparingly by Traherne and they are seldom striking. Typically, the comparisons are more often conceptual than visual.

An image that is repeated more than once, in both metaphor and simile, is the mirror. Examples are, from 'The Preparative':

> Pure Empty Powers that did nothing loath,
>   Did like the fairest Glass,
>   Or Spotless polisht Brass,
> Themselvs soon in their Objects Image cloath;
> (11.51–4)

and from 'Amendment':

> And is my Soul a Mirror that must Shine
> Even like the Sun, and be far more Divine?
> (11.34–5)

The mirror is a closed image, endlessly reflecting back upon itself. The affinities with hermeticism are obvious as is the similar notion of Creation as an endless circle.

Another device, so rare that one wonders if Traherne ever uses it intentionally, is alliteration. An example from 'Wonder' produces one of Traherne's more lyric lines:

> The Skies in their Magnificence,
> The Lively, Lovely Air.
> (11.9–10)

This is more than alliteration in that the same consonants are repeated with a change of vowel sounds. The unexpected order of the adjectives may add to the effect. Philip Traherne altered it to 'lovly lively Air', the more usual order in English but less musically effective. The two lines taken together derive some of their poetic quality from the word *Magnificence*. The Latinate word, used in collocation with the native *Skies*, has an amplitude that matches the concept.

Paradox is an intrinsic part of Traherne's verse, as it is of his total meaning. In this sense it is not the same as the riddling or word play of the other metaphysical poets. The very heart of his subject matter is paradoxical: time and eternity, end and beginning, physical and spiritual, even good and apparent evil – these the poet shows are ultimately one and the same. The syntactical complexities of paradox were examined in the analysis of a stanza from 'The Anticipation'. Paradox accounts, too, for the constant repetitions of words such as *End*; *Means*; *Fountains*; *Eternitie* and many others. A word that occurs once only and is nearer to the word play of the other poets is the modifier *Yesterdays-yet-present* ('Thoughts. I.'). This, too, is a multiple compound and compound words, except for the common ones (not punctuated as such), are almost totally absent from Traherne's language.

One important use of imagery remains. At the very close of the sequence Traherne introduces a luxuriant type of imagery that is quite different from that used hitherto. The sensuousness of *Soft and Swelling grapes*, a typical biblical image, used also by Herbert; *precious Seas/ Of Nectar and Ambrosia*' ; and the *Lillies* with their *pleasant Odors* differ markedly from the restraint of the previous poems and must be deliberate. The early poems are linked to the senses but without any of the sensuousness often associated with them. At this climax to the spiritual journey of the soul taste, sight, hearing and smell return with a richness that comes from language and symbols that are either biblical or traditionally Christian.

One concept that impinges on various aspects of Traherne's language has been left to the end. This is the 'circle', which is central to the constant interaction between God and man. Images and ideas based on circles or spheres occur in all the metaphysical poets from Donne onwards. The sphere was a means of viewing the world and universe from Elizabethan times and it persists in the poetry examined here. It is indeed a recurring image that links the poets together and lies at the heart of the cyclical nature of their notion of the universe, particularly that of Vaughan and Traherne. In none is the idea of the circle more central than in Traherne. At the beginning of the sequence the infant soul is seen as surrounded by the natural world, at the centre of the circle, and ignorant as yet of anything beyond:

> I was an Adam there,
> A little Adam in a Sphere
> Of Joys! O there my Ravisht Sence
> Was entertaind in Paradice,
> And had a Sight of Innocence.
> ('Innocence' 11.51–5)

The word *Sphere* is one of the group of nouns denoting this concept of the circle. Others are *circle* itself; *orb*; *globe* and also *point*. They appear whenever this theme is paramount in the poetry. Another related noun is *eye*.

In its state of innocence the soul is all *Ey*, which is

> the Sphere
> Of all Things ...
> ('The Improvment' 11.23–4)

In other words, the eye, the chief organ of the senses in Traherne's poetry, encompasses or encircles everything. This is expressed more fully earlier in the sequence of poems in 'The Preparative':

> Then was my Soul my only All to me,
>   A Living Endless Ey,
>   Far wider then the Skie
> Whose Power, whose Act, whose Essence was to see.
>   (11.11–14)

The same idea is expressed by Donne in *The Second Anniversarie*. The soul, having left the body after death 'is growne all Ey' (1.200). The sense is similar to Traherne's. Without the encumbrance of the physical senses the soul can perceive directly and completely. 'The Preparative' continues to use more explicit 'circle' words:

> I was an Inward *Sphere of Light*,
> Or an Interminable Orb of *Sight*,
>   An Endless and a Living Day,
> *A vital Sun* that round about did *ray*
>   All Life, and Sence,
> A Naked Simple Pure *Intelligence*.
>   (11.15–20)

Unlike Donne's description of the soul after death the *Intelligence* at this infant stage is not intellectual and cognitive but, paradoxically, wholly of the senses. In 'My Spirit' Traherne extends this notion of the soul as a receptive 'sphere' to the idea of its being at one with the objects it perceives. This involves him in the paradox that it is both at the heart and at the circumference of the circle:

> But being Simple like the Deitie
>   In its own Centre is a Sphere
> Not shut up here, but evry Where.
>
> It Acts not from a Centre to
>   Its Object as remote,
> But present is, when it doth view,
> Being with the Being it doth note.
>   (11.15–21)

The physical and the senses are transcended, but not left behind, since physical objects, which had been rejected just before, finally take their part too in the ceaseless and unbroken round:

> Fowls Fishes Beasts Trees Herbs and precious flowers,
> Seeds Spices Gums and Aromatick Bowers
> ...
> ... offer up themselves as Gifts of Love.
> ('Thoughts. IV.' 11.47–51)

Here again Traherne shows the influence of hermetic thought and the Cambridge Platonists. Man goes beyond the physical world around him by power of intellect. It is no accident that at the end of the sequence four of the poems are entitled 'Thoughts'. The first states clearly the superiority of mind over the physical side of man:

> The Ey's confind, The Body pent
> In narrow Room: Lims are of small Extent.
> But Thoughts are always free.
> And as they're best,
> So can they even in the Brest,
> Rove ore the World with Libertie:
> Can Enter Ages, Present be
> In any Kingdom, into Bosoms see.
> Thoughts, Thoughts can come to Things, and view,
> What Bodies cant approach unto.
> They know no Bar, Denial, Limit, Wall:
> But have a Liberty to look on all.
> (' Thoughts. I.' 11.61–72)

Thus the vocabulary of the early poems, with its insistence on physical attributes and 'limiting' or 'confining' words, returns.

The sequence ends in rapt contemplation of God's goodness. Through means of a selective vocabulary, Traherne has brought his theme full circle, with a new and deeper meaning infused into the same emotion as he expressed at the beginning in 'The Salutation'. Traherne's whole theme reaches behind and beyond the physical objects to their universal and spiritual implications.

In this sense, although not the greatest, he is perhaps the most consistently metaphysical, in one sense of the word, of all metaphysical poets.

7 Analysis of Passages

Donne's best-known lyrics have been much analysed. His *Verse Letters* are less known and a passage from one of them has therefore been chosen for examination here. Between 1608 and her death in 1627 Donne wrote at least eight Verse Letters to Lucy, Countess of Bedford, patroness and friend to many of the best poets of the day. Most of these belong to the years 1609–14. The first five stanzas of 'To the Countess of Bedford at New Year's Tide' show many of the characteristics of Donne's writing. They combine the intimate and formal, as befits a poet addressing his patron:

1   This twilight of two yeares, not past nor next,
        Some embleme is of mee, or I of this,
    Who Meteor-like, of stuffe and forme perplext,
        Whose *what*, and *where*, in disputation is,
5   If I should call mee *any thing*, should misse.

    I summe the yeares, and mee, and finde mee not
        Debtor to th'old, nor Creditor to th'new,
    That cannot say, My thankes I have forgot,
        Nor trust I this with hopes, and yet scarce true
10   This bravery is, since these times shew'd mee you.

    In recompence I would show future times
        What you were, and teach them to'urge
                towards such,
    Verse embalmes vertue; and Tombs, or Thrones of rimes,
        Preserve fraile transitory fame, as much

15   As spice doth bodies from corrupt aires touch.
           Mine are short-liv'd; the tincture of your name
              Creates in them, but dissipates as fast
           New spirits; for, strong agents with the same
              Force that doth warme and cherish, us doe wast;
20   Kept hot with strong extracts, no bodies last:

           So, my verse built of your just praise, might want
              Reason and likelihood, the firmest Base,
           And made of miracle, now faith is scant,
              Will vanish soone, and so possesse no place,
25   And you, and it, too much grace might disgrace.

Donne's syntax is at its most compressed and elliptical. The vocabulary presents little difficulty although, because of the semi-formal style of address (the formal pronoun *you* takes the place of the intimate *thou*, which Donne normally uses for lovers in *Songs and Sonets*), there is a sprinkling of words of Latin and French origin. Even so, native words outnumber them by about five to one and there are, as usual in Donne, whole lines (e.g. 11.6 and 9) of monosyllabic words.

    The poet begins by drawing attention to himself as he stands poised between the 'two yeares'. This uncertainty about position is expressed by the typical Donne interrogatives: *what* and *where* in line 4. These come in a simile drawn from astronomy, a subject of topical interest. The simile is introduced by a compressed compound: *Meteor-like*. This links the two objects compared, the meteor and the poet, more closely than is usual in simile. In the second stanza the poet decides that he owes nothing to the past and can expect nothing of the future. A swift reversal is then introduced with the double conjunction *and yet*. In the final line and a half of the stanza he disclaims his assessment of the past year and shifts the focus from himself to the addressee: *since these times shew'd mee you*. The apparent awkwardness of two juxtaposed pronouns at the end of the line is typical of Donne. Not only does it foreground *you* by its end position and stress but also places poet and patroness in dramatic relationship.

    The next stanzas consider the commemorative value of verse. A second simile, drawn from the custom of embalming, is followed by another of topical interest from alchemy. This contains the most detailed and extended analogy of the three similes and, like the others, it uses Romance and specifically Latin vocabulary. The fourth stanza says that the essence of his patroness's being is so strong that it may ultimately destroy the verse in which the poet seeks to preserve it, just as alchemical agents, if too powerful, burn and destroy the substance which they initially sustain. Hence, his verse, based on the miraculous in alchemy may, in this time of scepticism, vanish and so 'disgrace' the very graciousness that he is commemorating. The extract ends with this typical paradox, conveyed through the rhetorical figure of *polyptoton*, with the juxtaposition of *grace* and *disgrace*.

Obscurity rises from Donne's use of grammatical words, especially pro-forms. The grammatical words, usually thought 'empty', are essential to meaning in Donne's dialectic and give it its distinctive energy.

As is usual, personal pronouns do not function as pro-forms in most places. Initially first person singular pronouns dominate as the poet concentrates on his own condition. The subject form *I* is slightly less prominent (not numerically less) than the oblique *me*, because the grammatical subject is of less significance than the semantic subject indicated sometimes by *I* but more often by *me*. *Me* receives full stress twice, once in line 2 and again in line 6. Both instances come at mid-line before the caesura. *I* is stressed clearly only once in line 2 where it is chiastically balanced with *me*. The second person *you* is fully stressed at the end of the second stanza on its first appearance. This indicates the shift of focus. On its second occurrence, in line 12, it is unstressed, the emphasis here being on the essential nature of the Countess, which is conveyed in the verb form *were*. The stressed position of the pronoun in the last line of the extract closes this transitional passage by drawing attention once more to the subject of the poem. An absolute use of the possessive pronoun *Mine* occurs in line 16 and there is an instance of *it* in the final line. Both pronouns refer deictically to the poet's verse, although *it* refers unambiguously to the word *verse* itself (1.21) and *Mine* refers strictly to *Tombs, or Thrones of rimes* at the end of line 13, since it is followed by the plural verb *are*. *Verse* occurs at the beginning of the same line and is included in the meaning. In these two instances the personal pronouns are pro-forms and as such they add to the elliptical quality of the extract. Their reference is not immediately clear because they are in both cases some distance away from the noun for which they substitute.

Demonstrative pronouns functioning as pro-forms add further to the compression and difficulty of unravelling meaning. At the end of the second line the referent of *this* is not altogether clear. It could be 'This twilight of two years' and, indeed, that seems at first to make most sense, but the other possibility: 'Some embleme', is probably intended because of the chiastic construction of the line. In line 8 the initial *That* substitutes for *th'old*, itself an ellipsis for 'the old year'. *This* in the following line, meaning *the new*, similarly represents 'the new year'. Here adjectives unusually take on the function of pro-forms and this increases the range of Donne's elliptical forms. A similar usage comes in the first line, in which *past* and *next* also imply an entire nominal group. *Such*, as mentioned in the chapter on Donne (pp.31–2), sometimes functions like a demonstrative. An instance occurs at the end of line 12. This is a good example of the pro-form *such* not used as part of a simile as so often it is. It refers back directly to the clause 'What you were'. All these instances of demonstrative pro-forms as well as *such* are in stressed positions. The resulting ellipses and the need to search back through the poem to find referents add to the semantic difficulty.

Little importance attaches to verbs functioning as pro-forms in this extract. Nor does it to lexically full forms of primary auxiliaries. Forms of the verb *be* are used sparingly. *Is* occurs twice in a stressed position but neither time does it greatly affect the meaning of the poem. The first instance, at the end of line 4, is further emphasized by inversion of the adverbial adjunct and verb. This, related to the notion of the poet's 'being', which he is questioning, has more significance than the second instance in line 10, although this also receives stress. *Were* in line 12 is more integrated into the meaning. It confirms the 'essential being' of the poet's patroness, the 'essence' with which he is concerned. Even though attention is further drawn to the verb by the reference of *such* at the end of the line, however, the emphasis is not as striking as it sometimes is in Donne's poems. Perhaps this is because the subject is not picked up in the stanzas immediately following. Only one auxiliary functioning as a pro-form occurs in this passage. At line 15 *doth* substitutes for the full verbal group 'doth preserve'. This is easily understood and is not stressed. In passing we may note the lexically empty *do* in *doe wast* in line 19. This is not an instance of emphatic *do* and is the one truly 'lexically empty' word in the extract.

The syntax of this extract includes both the normal English S V C order of statements that is typical of *Songs and Sonets* and the more complex clause structure of some of Donne's longer poems. Complexity in the first and last stanzas, with inversion, embedding and subordination, results in both cases in a clause complex that takes up the entire stanza. The fourth stanza, which is closely linked to the fifth by the conjunction *so*, also has some inversion and embedding. The other stanzas (two and three) have short co-ordinate clauses and are much simpler. Occasionally there is no conjunction and clauses are simply juxtaposed. There is no syntactic link between lines 10 and 11 after the change of direction in the final clause of the second stanza. The break is only syntactic, however: semantically the clause follows on with the initial phrase 'In recompense', a typical example of Donne's pursuing a train of thought through juxtaposed statements.

As might be expected, all three similes involve slightly longer and more complex clauses. The first, in the first stanza, is preceded by a resumptive *who*, which introduces a relative clause. This is then suspended until after the simile and a short embedded conditional clause. The stanza also includes much inversion and also chiasmus in the extremely compressed second line. *I of this* is elliptical not only by reason of the pro-form *this* but because the verb is omitted and has to be 'understood' from the preceding clause. The final stanza is complicated more by embedding than inversion. The main co-ordinate clauses run: 'So my verse ... might want/ Reason and likelihood ... And ... will vanish soon ... And you, and it, too much grace might disgrace'. The only inversion comes in this final clause and complicates an otherwise straightforward but highly contrived rhetorical statement. In this clause the two conjoined complements *you* and *it* are thematic,[1] and Donne thereby foregrounds his 'verse', the focus of the three preceding stanzas, as well as his patroness, the subject of the whole poem towards whom he will shortly direct the reader's attention.

Through alternation of complex and simple clause structure the syntax mirrors the various moods of the passage. The note of uncertainty in two of the stanzas is conveyed by inverted and embedded clauses, as well as by rhetorical figures. The statement 'now faith is scant' is indicative of the times in which Donne was writing. We might compare the confident assertion of Shakespeare when engaged on a similar exercise:

> Not marble nor the gilded monuments
> Of princes shall outlive this powerful rhyme,
> But you shall shine more bright in these contents
> Than unswept stone besmeared with sluttish time.
> (Sonnet 55, 1–4)

or:

> So long as men can breathe or eyes can see,
> So long lives this, and this gives life to thee.
> (Sonnet 18, 13–14)

Shakespeare had no doubt about the durability of his verse – a theme common in classical poetry. Donne lived in an age when questioning had begun to take the place of assertion. This uncertainty shows in the texture of his verse, which, like the image of the meteor, is almost always 'of stuff and form perplexed'. The ways in which Donne conveys his meaning through language are hallmarks of the metaphysical mode of writing.

The language of Vaughan's 'Unprofitablenes' differs in kind from that used in the extract from Donne. In contrast the meaning is immediately clear, even though it is conveyed throughout by metaphor:

> How rich, O Lord! how fresh thy visits are!
> 'Twas but Just now my bleak leaves hopeles hung.
>   Sullyed with dust and mud;
> Each snarling blast shot through me, and did share
> 5   Their Youth, and beauty, Cold showres nipt, and wrung
>   Their spiciness, and bloud;
> But since thou didst in one sweet glance survey
> Their sad decays, I flourish, and once more
>   Breath all perfumes, and spice;

10   I smell a dew like *Myrrh*, and all the day
     Wear in my bosome a full Sun; such store
         Hath one beame from thy Eys.
     But, ah, my God! what fruit hast thou of this?
     What one poor leaf did ever I yet fall
15   To wait upon thy wreath?
     Thus thou all day a thankless weed doest dress,
     And when th'hast done, a stench, or fog is all
         The odour I bequeath.

The poem is in three parts: the speaker's condition before the intervention of God; his revival as a result of God's regenerative power; and finally his ultimate failure to yield any return to his Creator. The theme is typical of Vaughan. The final state, in which man fails to make a due return to his Creator, haunted his imagination. He asked for the following words to be engraved on his tombstone: *Servus inutilis: peccator maximus hic iaceo* ('A useless servant: here I, the greatest sinner, lie').

The metaphor of the plant – at times it seems to be a tree but at the end it is specifically called a 'weed' – is implicit rather than overt. Typically it is taken from the natural world. By extension through the whole poem it becomes a miniature allegory. It also has an emblematic quality, although it is not a static emblem such as would have been found in the preceding century. There is, too, an emblematic-type image: 'all the day/ [I] Wear in my bosome a full Sun'. Without knowledge of the emblem tradition this seems a strange concept, incapable of apprehension or of being visualized. The extended metaphor of the plant makes for a consistency of texture and evenness that is often lacking in Vaughan's longer poems. Although this poem does not reach the heights of some of Vaughan's poetry, it never flags.

The syntax is straightforward. Typically, the poem opens with exclamations, although these are neither forceful nor abrupt.The movement of the verse is conversational, as often in Vaughan. The opening statement occupies the second and third lines. The pentameter followed by a three-stressed line creates a conversational tone, which makes initially for a leisurely pace. This is the longest clause in the poem. Subsequent clauses, although shorter, often run over lines and thus, with intervening short lines, reinforce the impression of speech.

In this poem it is vocabulary that enriches and deepens the meaning. Groups of words reflect Vaughan's main preoccupations. There are biblical echoes throughout. More obvious, however, are words taken from alchemy and hermeticism. Those which represent the divine spark or essence are *spice* and the derivative noun extended from the adjectival form, *spiciness*. Another is *dew* and, importantly, *Sun*, the source of life itself. *Glance* is also associated with the engendering essence and, by association, *beame* would seem to be drawn into the group. *Blood* is also associated with hermetic vocabulary. That these words cluster in the stanza in which the speaker experiences a revitalization is no accident.

Of greater semantic significance are the words drawn from nature. Vaughan uses three types of nature vocabulary, which he both conflates and juxtaposes (see pp.110–13). A combination of words may give a clear indication of which type predominates in any one place. In this poem two are used alternately and reflect the alteration in the speaker's condition. When he is in a state of original sin, the vocabulary is that of the ordinary natural world: *dust*; *mud*; *leaves*; *showers* and the evocation of wind in *snarling blast*. Once God has embraced man in his 'glance', however, the vocabulary changes. Nature words from the Bible appear: *perfumes*; *spice* and *Myrrh*, recalling the language of the Song of Songs. The mood changes again in the last six lines as the speaker contemplates once more his natural and unworthy state. The vocabulary, therefore, returns to that of the natural world of the opening. *Weed*; *stench* and *fog* are the only 'odour' – juxtaposition of the biblical-type word is deliberate – that he believes he can ultimately yield his Maker.

The types of word that are of most significance for the meaning of the poem, apart from the nouns already mentioned, are adjectives and verbs. Adjectives give the verse an immediate lift. In the first line both *rich* and *fresh* are heavily stressed. Adjectives, as has been pointed out, are relatively unusual in metaphysical poetry. Here, the use of *fresh* is particularly happy. The word itself is commonplace but its unusual placing in this context evokes, even if only half-consciously, all the associations of fresh air and an outdoor world. The spring-like quality of God is contrasted to the experience of man. *Bleak* in collocation with *leaves* in the following line is not only unforeseen but destroys the positive associations of *rich* and *fresh*. *Snarling* in line 4 follows up the wintry side of nature with an aggressive adjective that is vivid in its evocation of sight and sound. After this the adjectives diminish and are unremarkable. Their incidence at the outset, however, has already done its work.

The verbs also change in the different sections of the poem. At the beginning, the activity of the natural agents, wind and rain, is conveyed by the monosyllabic verbs *shot* and *nipt*. Both have short vowels and end with the voiceless plosive /t/. These sounds reinforce the meaning of *share*, an older variant of *shear* in the sense 'cut off'. It is monosyllabic and, by reason of the initial voiceless fricative, slightly onomatopoeic. It conjures up the sound of tearing or ripping. The final verb *wrung* is mimetic rather than onomatopaeic, the sound reflecting the movement. Other verbs connected with twisting movements, such as *wriggle* and *writhe*, begin with the orthographic combination *wr*, now pronounced simply /r/.[2] *Wrung* also has a short vowel. The dynamic and predominantly staccato verbs of this first part indicate the brutal force of nature in its malign or destructive aspect. In the middle section, as the nature words change, so too do the verbs. They attach to the speaker rather than to the natural objects and although mainly dynamic, differ in kind from the earlier ones. They are durative rather than momentary or punctual. *Flourish* is only marginally dynamic, being midway between a state and an action.[3] *Breathe* also, although classed as a dynamic verb, is an involuntary process and not strongly active. *Smell* is classified as a stative verb of inert perception. Finally, *wear* does not denote activity and in this context is not even the result of deliberate choice on the part of the subject but the result of God's regenerative powers. It is virtually drawn, therefore, into the midway category of 'stance' verbs, like *flourish*. Throughout this section the speaker is being worked on and the verbs, although not passives, more or less reflect this passivity. *Flourish* has two syllables and *breathe* a long vowel. Their final fricative consonants further lengthen the sound and help to create a sense of space. In this they are quite unlike the shorter verbs of the first part of the poem, which mainly end in voiceless stops. They are, like the earlier verbs, partly onomatopoeic.

The various strands of the vocabulary and the way in which they are deployed are the principal means by which Vaughan enriches his meaning and they give this poem its particular emphasis. The sound of the words, especially the verbs, underlines the sense the poet seeks to convey.

For Vaughan, sound is often of the first importance and can strike the reader before the meaning becomes clear. To end this examination of some details in the poetry, I will look at this feature in a short extract from one of the best-known poems, 'The Morning Watch':

> In what Rings,
> And *Hymning Circulations* the quick world
> Awakes, and sings;
> The rising winds,
> And falling springs,
> Birds, beasts, all things
> Adore him in their kinds.
> Thus all is hurl'd
> In sacred *Hymnes*, and *Order*, The great *Chime*
> And *Symphony* of nature.
>   (11.9–18)

These lines contain extended examples of assonance and 'consonantal chime'. The most frequently repeated vowel is /ɪ/, often followed by a nasal /n/ or /ŋ/. The diphthongs /eɪ/ and /aɪ/ also occur several times. These sounds establish a pattern in the reader's mind. They reach a climax with the word *Chime*, and this carries through into the first part of the following line with the word *Symphony*. The rhyme for *Chime* is outside the unit of meaning and almost beyond the range of the inner ear, since it comes six lines further on. Nevertheless, *Chime* reverberates on the ear because of the previous insistence on two of its three sounds, so that on a first reading the fact that it does not rhyme with a preceding word is likely to pass unnoticed. The reader experiences a sense of fulfilment and satisfaction. The word does indeed 'chime' in the mind as it draws the dominant sounds of the passage together in one word, like a chord that brings to a close a passage of music. Further assonance can be traced in the passage, especially in the repeated /ɜː/ of *Circulations*; *world*; *Birds*; *hurl'd* and *world* again. The lines are a web of interweaving sounds that harmonize the disparate parts of the world they are intended to signify. Thus meaning and sound are at one in a way which is peculiar to Vaughan and which makes up a considerable part of the overall appeal of his poetry, even when it is not as clearly demonstrable as it is in this extract.

8 Conclusion

There is no 'school' of Donne and yet it is of Donne that most people think when the word 'metaphysical' is mentioned in connection with poetry. Indeed, far more studies of Donne's poetry and individual poems have been written than of all the other metaphysical poets put together. If there were any 'school' of metaphysical poetry it might well have been the school of Herbert. It was for Herbert, not Donne, that both Crashaw and Vaughan expressed their admiration. Crashaw wrote some laudatory verses on Herbert's *The Temple* and entitled his first volume of religious poetry *The Steps to the Temple* after Herbert's work. Vaughan acknowledged the debt he owed Herbert in his Preface of 1655 and borrowed from him to an extent unsurpassed in the history of English literature. Herbert, himself, of course, knew Donne, whose 'The Autumnall' to Magdalen Herbert, the poet's mother, is among the best-known of his poems. Walton tells us that shortly before his death Donne had several seals made and engraved with an anchor as the emblem of hope. These he sent to his friends. One of the recipients was Herbert, and Donne's poem which, according to Walton accompanied the seal, was probably preserved among his papers along with some verses written by the younger man on receiving the present.[1] Traherne remains a rather isolated figure in this group. Writing some twenty years after Vaughan published his *Silex Scintillans*, and after the restoration of the monarchy, he would certainly have known the work of the other poets but the taste for meditative religious verse was already over and Traherne's poems were not published in his lifetime. Indeed after his brother's death they were lost and only came to light by accident. First published in 1903, they have still received much less attention than the poems of the others.

Even without Traherne, the continuity of these metaphysical poets stretches over sixty years, from Donne, who was writing as early as the 1590s, at the same time as Shakespeare was becoming established in London as its foremost playwright, to Vaughan writing in the 1650s. If we include Traherne we move on another twenty years. Traherne probably wrote most of his poetry, as well as his best prose, shortly before his death in 1673. This is an exceptionally long period for verse of similar styles and attitudes to persist. We have only to recall the gap between Georgian poetry of World War I and that being written at the end of the twentieth century to realize how unlikely it is that there should be such continuity. The disruption caused by war and uncertainty in this later period is not unlike that of the seventeenth century. The persistence of metaphysical religious poetry is remarkable.

That is not to say that all metaphysical poetry is the same. The wide variety of styles within one basic framework of subject matter and linguistic usage is evident from even a slight acquaintance with the work of the individual poets. One feature which they share is experimentation in stanza forms. Donne's metrical virtuosity in *Songs and Sonets* has often been remarked on. It has been calculated that he uses forty six different stanza forms, of which forty four occur only once.[2] Of the total only four were used before Donne and three copied by later poets.[3] If they did not copy Donne's particular stanza forms the later metaphysical poets devised a wide range of metrical patterns of their own. These help to account for the flexibility of their linguistic usage, which allowed the sense of a speaking voice and the dramatic effects that are found to some extent in all the poets and most obviously in Donne, Herbert and Vaughan. It is not always realized that Herbert's 'The Collar', for instance, is in free verse. There is no regular metrical pattern throughout the thirty six lines. The poem is held together by rhyme and other cohesive devices, not least the rhythmic control that sweeps the poem along to its unexpected reversal in the final lines. Several of Crashaw's longer poems follow no regular metrical pattern. 'In the Glorious Epiphanie' and 'On the Assumption' are two examples. Conversely, Traherne, who writes a sort of free poetic prose, adheres strictly to his very intricate stanza forms and metres in the poetry, even though much of his verse has the expository nature of a prose thesis. This can result in a less lyric and musical poetry than that of his predecessors. The rhymes do not chime so satisfyingly on the ear as they do, say, in Herbert's poems. The lines often run over and are less clearly marked rhythmically than those of Herbert. The very variety of stanza forms makes for differences in the poetry of the metaphysical poets.

Common features in the language of these poets are more easily identified than differences. There are exceptions to any generalizations as the reader will recognize. Diction tends to be simple and plain, following the move in the early seventeenth century towards a plainer type of language than that used by the Elizabethan courtly poets. Much vocabulary is monosyllabic and derives from native sources. The number of Latinate and Romance words varies in individual poets but all rely heavily on Germanic vocabulary. The strength of the poems lies in nouns and verbs rather than adjectives, which are often commonplace or tend to be abstract. The poetry is not descriptive although it contains some very visual elements, especially in the emblems used. Syntax is usually straightforward. Clauses tend to be shorter rather than longer and clause complexes are generally right-branching, dependent clauses following after the main clause. Inversion of the basic elements (S V C) within clauses is the exception rather than the norm. This is not to say that the sense is always easy to follow. Because the poets favour ellipsis and compression, as well as paradox and frequent amibiguities of reference, the reader encounters difficulty more frequently than might be expected. This is compounded by the use of conceits, which are often thought to be the hallmark of metaphysical writing. There is extensive use of metaphor and symbolic writing, which can obscure meaning even when its intention is to be ultimately precise and exact. These are some of the features of language which most of the poets share to a greater or lesser extent. They are all found in Donne and Herbert and some at least in each of the three later poets.

If, because they are discrete linguistic features that can be named, similarities lend themselves to listing, the differences are less easily defined. Yet differences there are, sufficient to make the voice of each poet distinct and instantly recognizable. One would not mistake a poem of Crashaw for one of Donne, or ascribe one of Herbert's poems to Traherne. Neither is there much danger of confusing Vaughan and Herbert, in spite of Vaughan's copious borrowings. Whatever common linguistic ground these poets share, the resulting poetry is highly individual. The aspects of language that most readily disclose the differences are vocabulary and imagery. The tendency for all five poets, with the possible exception of Traherne, is towards a simple native-based vocabulary that is essentially concrete. This too is in line with the move towards a plain unornamented style that characterizes the language of Donne and Herbert in particular. They start from a concrete proposition or image and by a process of reasoning and logic move towards an intellectual or spiritual conclusion. One meaning of the term 'metaphysical' is going beyond or behind the physical. This starting point in the concrete physical world should not surprise us. Each of the poets does this in some way and it is their individual manipulation of the language to this end that results in such widely different poetry, although it is still contained within a comparatively narrow compass of subject matter and attitudes.

Donne's concreteness resides in his images. From these he develops the logical arguments that characterize metaphysical verse. In *Songs and Sonets* these do not always result in an intellectual conclusion. The end of the argument may be as concrete and physical as the metaphor which is the vehicle. There has been much argument over Donne's purpose in such poems as 'The Flea' and 'The Exstasie' but whether they are poems of seduction or not matters little or, indeed, if the end is physical or intellectual. The poetry and the poems exist in the reasoning which stems from the concrete images. This is true of all the lyrics in *Songs and Sonets*, most of which are essentially about the nature of love and the act of loving. The same type of logical argument runs through all Donne's poetry and extends to the *Holy Sonnets* and the other handful of religious short poems.

Herbert's poems are even more firmly rooted in the everyday world than Donne's. He takes the emblems and images of his metaphors from his physical surroundings and, like Donne, builds up logical arguments on them. His purpose is spiritual, although in his thinking this was almost certainly as concrete as any physical end. His poetry, with Vaughan's, is the most intensely personal of all this group of poets, even when he adopts a *persona* or dramatizes his subject. Virtually every poem explores the relationship between man and God and it is to the discovery of the nature of this relationship that his concrete images lead.

When we turn to Crashaw, the concrete language and imagery appear to be inverted. Rather than leading his readers towards a spiritual conclusion, Crashaw seems to translate the spiritual into the physical world that can be understood through the senses. Although he employs all the devices of paradox, ellipsis and verbal repetition, the resulting poetry is contemplative and devotional rather than logical and reasoning. It is as if he stands back and watches the great drama of the Christian faith unfold before him and describes its mysteries in concrete terms and imagery. This accounts for his greater use of colourful and descriptive adjectives that make their appeal to the senses and is one of the reasons for the peculiarly Catholic feel of his poetry and for its being labelled 'baroque'.

Although Vaughan also uses emblematic images and symbols that have their basis in concrete vocabulary, he often takes natural objects in a literal sense and by no means always uses them as a vehicle for argument. Vaughan sees the infinite in the world around him and makes the transition to the spiritual dimension in a flash of insight that has earned him the name of visionary. It is this intuitive apprehension of divinity that he often conveys in his poetry. He sees 'heaven in a grain of sand' and the two worlds fuse instantaneously. There is no space for him between the concrete and the ghostly, between time and eternity.

For Traherne, on the other hand, the concrete and physical are very definitely the literal means through which man apprehends his Creator and by a process of reasoning progresses beyond the limitations of the physical body to attain the heights of divine wisdom. Whereas in Vaughan's poetry, and also in that of Herbert and Crashaw, the literal and the metaphorical are often so intertwined that they cannot be disentangled, in Traherne the metaphorical disappears almost entirely. On the other hand, his vocabulary, even when concrete (and he tends to a greater use of abstract and learned words), is more general than that of the other poets. When Vaughan mentions 'some drowsie silk-worme' ('Resurrection and Immortality') this is an individual animal even though he uses an indefinite albeit assertive determiner; when

Herbert calls night 'thy ebony box' ('Even-song') or draws attention to 'that square & speckled stone' of the floor which is the emblem for *Patience* ('The Church-floore') we feel that he is seeing a particular box and floor; and when Crashaw, using a definite determiner that is nevertheless generic, speaks of 'The primrose's pale cheek' ('The Weeper') there is still the sense of a very concrete and strongly visualized flower. Traherne, however, nearly always names concrete objects in the plural, very often with no article, as in *Lips or Hands or Eys or Ears* ('The Salutation') and, with increasing generality, *Hedges, Ditches, Limits, Bounds* ('Wonder'). These are so little particularized that they tend to be assimilated into his more abstract vocabulary and are mere counters used for the sake of argument. Traherne still relies heavily on paradox (inevitably since paradox lies at the heart of Christian faith) but elaboration rather than ellipsis marks his verse. Compared with Vaughan's instantaneous grasp of the spiritual his process of reasoning seems plodding and laborious. But he, too, although in a completely different way from any of the other poets, begins from the concrete and works towards the spiritual.

In different ways each of these five poets uses the concrete to explore and convey his understanding of the spiritual or divine. This necessitates a basis of concrete vocabulary and imagery. It is the variations played on these that produce poetry of such individual kinds.

To draw conclusions about the language of the five poets presents grave difficulties. The similarities of language and linguistic use are obvious to the extent of making an examination of their work run the danger of being repetitious. Yet, in spite of common ground, the differences ensure that the poetry of each is quite distinct. The language of their poetry, linked for the most part by a common subject matter, is like a set of variations upon a theme. This makes for infinite variety not only in the language but in the perspectives it throws upon the theme itself – a variety that no 'custom' of repeated readings can ever 'stale'.

Appendix 1
Hermetic Philosophy

Hermetic philosophy goes back to earliest times and was known to the ancient Egyptians and the Hebrews. By the mid seventeenth century it was complex and incorporated many Elizabethan ideas, such as the 'chain of being' and the relation of man to the universe as 'microcosm' and 'macrocosm'. It stressed the unity of the cosmos and the interdependence of all its parts. Hermeticism was linked to Christian doctrine by positing the divine essence inherent in all Creation. The divine part of man is his soul, but other living creatures are also endowed with a divine spark that keeps them in harmony or sympathy with God. Nor is this touch of the divine essence confined to animate beings. All things strive to be at one with God. This belief lies behind such lines by Vaughan as the following

> *Waters* that fall
> Chide, and fly up; *Mists* of corruptest fome
> Quit their first beds & mount; trees, herbs, flowres, all
> Strive upwards stil;
> ('The Tempest', 11.25–8)

and:

> So hills and valleys into singing break,
> And though poor stones have neither speech nor tongue,
> While active winds and streams both run and speak,
> Yet stones are deep in admiration.
> ('The Bird' 11.13–16)

Vaughan practised medicine on hermetic principles and translated a treatise on the subject written by Henry Nollius and first published in 1613: *Hermetical Physick: or, The right way to preserve, and to restore Health*. Vaughan's translation was published in 1655, the same year as the second part of *Silex Scintillans*. Hermetic medicine was based on a knowledge of correspondences or 'sympathetic' ties between different species. Diseases were cured by those substances, particularly herbs and plants, that had properties akin to the ailment. This follows the teaching of Paracelsus rather than the Galen tradition of the 'humours', on which most Elizabethan medical practice was based. Galen advocated applying the opposite humour to that which was believed to have caused the illness. This was supposed to correct the physical imbalance brought about by excess of one humour. There are references to Galen as well as Paracelsus in Donne. Herbert alludes to the Paracelsian tradition in his poem 'Man':

> Herbs gladly cure our flesh; because that they
>   Finde their acquaintance there.
>   (11.23–4)

Correspondences between various planes of being were part of the Elizabethan world view. The notion embraces the Elizabethan belief of man as the microcosm which parallels the macrocosm of the universe. Donne refers to it in one of the *Holy Sonnets*:

> I am a little world made cunningly
> Of elements, and an angel sprite.
>   (11.1–2)

It is essentially this belief that Herbert utilizes in 'Man', in which he says man 'is in little all the sphere' (1.22). As the quotation above demonstrates Herbert linked it more closely to hermetic philosophy than Donne. He expresses fully, albeit unconsciously, the relation between the Elizabethan and hermetic views:

>   Man is all symmetrie,
> Full of proportions, one limbe to another,
>   And all to all the world besides:
>   Each part may call the furthest, brother:
> For head with foot hath private amitie,
>   And both with moons and tides.
>   (11.13–18)

The 'symmetrie' and correspondence to which Herbert draws attention lie at the heart of the metaphysical conceits and ideas that characterize not only Vaughan's poetry but that of the group of poets examined in this book.

Another hermetic belief was that things change, merging into one another and re-emerging in different forms. All matter is thus in a state of flux. Here again is Herbert:

> As a young exhalation, newly waking,
> Scorns his first bed of dirt, and means the sky;
> But cooling by the way, grows pursie and slow,
> And setling to a cloud, doth live and die
> In that dark state of tears ...
> ('The Answer', 11.8–12)

The heat of the sun draws vapour upward from the earth, which, cooling in the upper atmosphere, falls again as rain. This is one of the cyclical patterns in nature. Another example of flux comes in 'The Book', a poem at the end of the Second Part of Vaughan's *Silex Scintillans*. The leaves of the book are followed through the stages of grass and linen, to paper; and the cover from the animal in the field to the leather binding. A parallel *perpetuum mobile* is apparent in man's restlessness, to which the poems repeatedly refer.

Various aspects of the doctrines of hermeticism are contained in Donne's *First Anniversarie*, in which Donne refers to them in the context of the world of the 'Egyptian Mages':

> What Artist now dares boast that he can bring
> Heaven hither, or constellate any thing,
> So as the influence of those starres may bee
> Imprisond in an Herbe, or Charme, or Tree,
> And doe by touch, all which those starres could do?
> The art is lost, and correspondence too.
> For heaven gives little, and the earth takes lesse,
> And man least knowes their trade, and purposes.
> If this commerce twixt heaven and earth were not
> Embarr'd, and all this trafique quite forgot,
> Shee, for whose losse we have lamented thus,
> Would worke more fully'and pow'rfully on us.

> Since herbes, and roots by dying, lose not all,
> But they, yea Ashes too, are medicinall
> Death could not quench her vertue so, but that
> It would be (if not follow'd) wondred at.
> (11.391–406)

The one legacy of hermetic philosophy still in daily use is the common phrase 'hermetically sealed'. It derives from the notion of a unity binding the cosmos together and would have particularly appealed to Vaughan, and also to Traherne.

Appendix 2
The Cambridge Platonists

Whereas hermetic philosophy seems to have had some influence on most of the metaphysical poets, the platonism associated with the Cambridge Platonists affected Traherne only. It was in part one of the answers to the materialism of Hobbes, whose *Leviathan* was not published until 1651. The Cambridge Platonists were a group of Cambridge scholars who, besides rejecting Hobbes, eschewed dogmatism in general. Joseph Glanvill (1636–80) who, although like Traherne an Oxford man, is associated with the group and also with the Royal Society, called his first and still best-known work *The Vanity of Dogmatizing* (1661). Following the lead of Benjamin Whichcote (1606–83), the Cambridge Platonists began to question the authority of traditional theology which had been handed down from the medieval Church Fathers and, above all, from Aquinas. Where they felt it was too rigid they believed it ought to be set aside. It had caused bloodshed and Civil War. If any lasting stability was to be attained, dogma should be abandoned. The scientific enquiry of the time led them to discard more and more beliefs that could not be scientifically upheld. They adapted the rational approach of Descartes (1596–1650) to spiritual matters. Their chief tenet was that man was endowed with reason by God and that this reason ('the candle of the Lord') would enable him to recognize the existence of his Creator and incline him to virtue. They maintained that everyone should be free to worship after his own manner and that the traditional forms of worship were not sacrosanct.

Traherne, being an Oxford man, was not strictly one of the group although, after he joined the household of Sir Orlando

Bridgeman, he would almost certainly have come in contact with some of the members, even if he had not already started to think along the same lines. In several respects he differs from the Cambridge group. Although a scholar and an intellectual, he never became overwhelmed with detail as some of the Cambridge men tended to be. Not spending his life in the seclusion of a university college, Traherne was able to practise his beliefs in the ordinary workaday world. This he did with whole-hearted zest. He did not dwell on death, evil and the inevitable wickedness of the flesh but rather exulted in man's corporeal state and the material substance of the natural world in which he is placed. These were the means through which man could come to knowledge of God. He believed completely in a God manifest and immanent in His creation. He also believed that if a man actively pursued joy or 'felicity', he would reach a spiritual condition in which he would see everything anew with the vision of God himself. Such beliefs shine through his poems and poetic prose.

Notes

Where full bibliographical details of a book are not included in the notes they will be found in the bibliography.

Chapter 1

1. See Hutchinson, *Henry Vaughan*, pp.156–64.
2. See Peterson, *The English Lyric from Wyatt to Donne*, p.118.
3. See Peterson, pp.166–7 and p.353.
4. Martines, *Society and History in English Renaissance Verse* says: 'The current of "plain and vigorous and sometimes violent diction" to be found in Donne ... is often closely associated with the life and temper of the Inns in the 1590s and early years of the seventeenth century', p.26 & *passim*.
5. 'A shepheard's tale' is an unfinished poem, written at the same time as *Astrophil and Stella*, 1581–3. It was inserted into the 1593 ed. of *Arcadia* by Mary Herbert, Countess of Pembroke. It is usually omitted from modern edns. It has more to do with Elizabethan pastoral than *Arcadia*, which is a courtly romance.
6. *Wires* was a term of praise in Elizabethan and Jacobean poetry. The word is used in this positive sense by Spenser in his *Epithalamion*. *Black*, however, is derogatory. All courtly heroines had golden hair.
7. For translation and composition of epigrams in schools see T. W. Baldwin, *William Shakespeare's Small Latine & Lesse Greeke*, 2 vols (Urbana: University of Illinois Press, 1944). In Vol. 1 he describes both the Winchester and the Eton systems in the 1560s. At both schools the boys began to study epigrams in the 4th form at the age of 13 or 14 years.
8. Andrea Alciati's *Emblematum Liber* published in Italy in 1531 was the first emblem book to be printed. It was in manuscript at least ten years earlier.
9. Freeman, p.3. For more details about the emblem tradition see Freeman, *English Emblem Books* and Sloane, *The Visual in Metaphysical Poetry*.
10. Quarles, *Emblemes* (1635), drew on the Jesuit tradition of emblem writing. The style is narrative and many of the pictures show

Anima (the Soul) in various adventures on her pilgrimage to heaven. Another figure, *Amor* (Love), cajoles, upbraids and assists. See Sloane, pp.24–7; 50–5.

Chapter 2

The texts used here are the four volumes of Donne's poetical works in the Oxford English Texts series, edited by Helen Gardner and W. Milgate.

1. Milgate's note (p.199) cites the *OED*: 'trunk' sb.14, 'perspective trunk, telescope'. He continues: 'Donne had read of the telescope in Galileo's *Sidereus Nuncius* (1610) ... ; he calls the telescope "Optick glasses" in *Sermons* iii.210¹'. The telescope was invented in Holland c.1608. Galileo made his c.1609. See also 'A Letter to the Lady Carey, and Mrs Essex Riche' 11.55–7 for a reference to the subject of optical illusions.
2. William Harvey discovered the circulation of the blood c.1616.
3. See Partridge, *John Donne: Language and Style*, p.66. 'Three poems of *Songs and Sonets* appeared in print as songs, with musical settings, in Alphonso Ferrabosco's *Ayres* (1609), William Corkine's *Second Book of Ayres* (1612) and John Dowland's *A Pilgrim's Solace* (1612): they were respectively *The Expiration, Breake of Day* and *Love's Infiniteness* (the last rewritten and entitled 'To ask for all thy love')'.
4. Bennett, *Four Metaphysical Poets*, p.42 & p.45, notes the number of monosyllables in Donne.
5. Josephine Miles, *Eras and Modes in English Poetry* (Berkeley & Los Angeles: California University Press, 1957), p.24, has calculated that Donne uses on average eight adjectives, sixteen nouns and twelve verbs in every ten lines of verse throughout his poetry. This is twice as many nouns as adjectives. But my calculations show that, apart from some of the *Elegie*s and *The First Anniversarie*, there are between three and five adjectives to every ten lines of verse (not counting premodifying nouns and numbers and possessives when nominal). This seems more what one would expect from the impression when reading the verse.
6. Winny, *A Preface to Donne*, pp.76–8, notes the way in which poets continued to accept the notion of three continents from ancient geographers in spite of the discovery of America by Columbus (1492). Donne refers to America in the Elegie, 'To his Mistris Going to Bed'.
7. This is based on Revelation VII.1: 'And after these things I saw four angels standing on the four corners of the earth, holding the four winds of the earth'. Donne added the seemingly contradictory image of the world as a globe, a concept which goes as far back as the sixth century B.C.
8. This is similar to several of Crashaw's extravagant images in 'The Weeper'. Quarles has an emblem which virtually illustrates this image. See p.95 and Chapter 4. n.7.

180 THE LANGUAGE OF THE METAPHYSICAL POETS

9. See Tillyard, *The Elizabethan World Picture*, Chapters 6 and 7, for the various types of correspondences.
10. Sister Miriam Joseph, *Rhetoric in Shakespeare's Time* (Columbia: Columbia University Press, 1947; repr. in a shortened version, New York: Harcourt, Brace & World Inc., (1962), p.307.
11. The explanation of this apparent puzzle lies in the fact that, in Helen Gardner's words:
> It is a Neo-Platonic commonplace that love makes 'of one person – two; and of two persons – one', and that 'two persons, who love each other mutually are not really two persons', but 'only one, or else four'.

(Gloss on 'The Extasie': *And makes both one, each this and that*, in *The Elegies and The Songs and Sonnets*, Commentary, p.183)

Chapter 3

The poems are quoted here from the Oxford English Texts, edited by F. E. Hutchinson (1941, repr. 1978).

1. See Tuve, *A Reading of George Herbert*, p.120 for a description of these and p.210 for editions and locations.
2. John Gerard, *The Herball or Generall Historie of Plantes* (1597), Bracken Books (from the edn of T.H. Johnson, 1636), 1985, pp.48–9 and 238–9.
3. Tuve, pp.128–9, notes that the comparison of the hole in Christ's side to a *saccus*, a bag for straining wine, was a known symbol. It had been used by Adam of St Victor. Herbert's conversion of the *saccus* to a letter bag seems to be original.
4. Noted by Edgecombe, *'Sweetnesse Readie Penn'd'*, p.103.
5. Thematic marking occurs when a group other than the subject is placed first in a clause, thereby focusing the reader's attention on it. Whatever comes first is called the 'theme' and this carries the main part of the 'message' or meaning.
6. Edgecombe, p.107. For a list of appositive sequences by other authors see E. B. Greenwood, "George Herbert's Sonnet 'Prayer': A Stylistic Study". *Essays in Criticism*, 15 (1965), 27–45.
7. See Edgecombe, pp.97–100 for a discussion of Herbert's language and the Collects.
8. Edgecombe, p.98.
9. For a detailed discussion of cohesion see M. A. K. Halliday and Ruqaiya Hasan, *Cohesion in English* (London: Longman, 1976).
10. See Halliday and Hasan, p.26.
11. Walter Nash, *Designs in Prose* (London: Longman, 1980), p.59.
12. See Tuve, p.145: 'The basic "concept" of the "conceit" quoted is the crucified Christ as a lyre, Love as music and just so in the *Speculum*

humanae salvationis "Christ was stendid [extended] on the crosse/ als in ane harpe ere the stringes" '. She includes a reproduction of an illustration from the *Speculum* in which pictures of Tubalcain and Jubal, the biblical discoverers of ironwork and music, are set side by side with the nailing of Christ on the cross (Plate XI) and notes that a similar one appears in the *Biblia Pauperum*.

    13. *Posy* with the meaning of an emblem survives into the eighteenth century, according to the *OED*. Herbert uses the word unequivocally in this sense in his poem 'The Posie'.

    14. See Edgecombe, pp.83–91 for more details of how repetition affects the meaning of a poem.

    15. Rugoff, *Donne's Imagery*, p.113.

Chapter 4

Crashaw's poems that are examined here are those in his *Steps to the Temple* (1646 & 1648) and *Carmen Deo Nostro* (1652). *Steps to the Temple* was first published in 1646. A second edition, which included further poems, appeared in 1648. *Carmen Deo Nostro* was published in 1652 and consisted chiefly of poems from the earlier two volumes. The poems are quoted here from the 1652 version where it exists. Otherwise they are from the 1646 edition, e.g. *Sospetto d'Herode*. One poem not published in Crashaw's lifetime, 'Oute of Grotius his Tragedy of Christes sufferinges' is also used for illustration. The text used is in the Oxford English Texts edited by L. C. Martin (2nd edition, 1957).

    1. *Sospetto d'Herode* is based on Marino's Italian poem, *La Strage de gli Innocenti* (?1610). See Martin's note, p.435.

    2. These are the readings set for the years 1631–5. See Parrish, *Richard Crashaw*, p.51ff.

    3. Wallerstein, *Richard Crashaw*, pp.125–6.

    4. Parrish notes this in relation to *Sospetto d'Herode*, pp.66–7.

    5. This seems a distinct improvement on the 1646 version:

    I saw th'officious Angels bring,
        The downe that their soft brests did strow,
    For well they now can spare their wings,
        When Heaven it selfe lyes here below.
    Faire Youth (said I) be not too rough,
    Thy Downe though soft's not soft enough.

    6. Milton would almost certainly have read Crashaw's poem. The first version of *Paradise Lost* was published in 1667, some twenty years after *Sospetto d'Herode*. Humphrey Moseley, who printed *Sospetto d'Herode*, first printed in 1645 some of Milton's early poems, including 'On the Morning of Christs Nativity'. For some verbal parallels of

182 THE LANGUAGE OF THE METAPHYSICAL POETS

Crashaw's poem in *Paradise Lost* see C. Schaar, 'The *Sospetto d'Herode* and *Paradise Lost*', *English Studies*, L (1969), 511–16.
    7. Quarles, *Emblemes* (1635), Book III, Emblem VIII.
    8. See Parrish, pp.160–4 for a detailed explanation of these lines.

Chapter 5

The text used here is the Oxford English Texts, edited by L. C. Martin (2nd edition, 1957). This is 'The second Edition, In two Books' of *Silex Scintillans* (1655), which included the first edition of 1650.

    1. For the term 'hermeticism' as used here and a fuller account of Vaughan's hermeticism see Appendix 1, pp.173–5.
    2. Rudrum connects *primros'd* with *Macbeth* and *Hamlet*: 'the primrose path of dalliance' (I.iii.50). See Rudrum, *Henry Vaughan: the Complete Poems*, p.529 n. The 'primrose path' has become proverbial, probably following Shakespeare. No earlier instance of this figurative use is recorded in the *OED*. Rudrum notes that Vaughan's use could also derive from Thomas Vaughan's *Lumen de Lumine*.
    3. See Hutchinson, *Henry Vaughan*, pp.158–9 for Vaughan's treatment of gender.
    4. For rhymes in Welsh poetry see Hutchinson, p.162.
    5. Assonance as used here indicates the repetition of vowel sounds. See G.N. Leech, *A Linguistic Guide to English Poetry*, (London: Longmans, Green & Co. Ltd, 1969) p.89ff. for various types of rhymes and sound patterns in words. For the influence of Vaughan's Welsh background on all these figures see Hutchinson, Chapter XII, pp.156–64.
    6. This is based on the Song of Songs, V.2.
    7. See Hutchinson, p.164, for 'cloathe the morning-starre with dust'.
    8. Psalm CIV.16. There is no mention of 'green' in the Geneva Bible, which we know Vaughan used (see Rudrum, p.539, n.54). The verse there reads: 'The high trees are satisfied, even the cedars of Lebanon, which hee hath planted'. The *AV* includes the word 'sap'. It seems likely that Vaughan was using both the Geneva Bible and the *AV* but not Coverdale's version of the Psalms, which is familiar to us from its inclusion in the *Book of Common Prayer* in 1662.
    9. Vaughan has taken the names *Cotswold* and *Cooper's* from literary sources. Two publications could have prompted the reference to *Cotswold*: Randolph's *Eclogue on the noble assemblies revived on Cotswold Hills, by Mr Robert Dover* or *Annalia Dubrensia. Upon the yearly celebration of Mr Robert Dover's Olympic Games upon Cotswold-Hills* (1636). Sir John Denham's *Cooper's Hill* was published in 1642.
    10. See Friedenreich, *Henry Vaughan*, pp.47–52 for a useful summary of the various positions critics have adopted in relation to Vaughan and 'nature'.
    11. Friedenreich, p.34, has also noted this reference and its implications for Vaughan's meaning.

12. See Rudrum, p.601 for the meaning of the second line. Freeman, *English Emblem Books*, pp.150–1, notes that the palm tree was an emblem signifying endurance.

Chapter 6

The poems of Traherne that are examined here are those in the Dobell Folio, which is in the Bodleian Library (MS. Eng. poet. c.42). This manuscript was discovered about 1888. At first it was thought the poems were the work of Vaughan but Traherne was identified as the author by Bertram Dobell, who published them in 1903. The Dobell Folio has the advantage of being in Thomas Traherne's own hand (with revisions added by Philip Traherne) and the spelling and punctuation are his. For language purposes, therefore, it is more authentic than the Burney MS., which was discovered and published by H. I. Bell in 1911. This is preserved in the British Library (Burney MS.392). It contains *Poems of Felicity*, which is the title given to his selection of the poems by Traherne's brother Philip, who prepared them for press after Thomas's death. Although many of the poems are the same in the two manuscripts, there are more in the Burney MS., and some in the Dobell MS. do not appear in Burney. The poems are quoted from the Dobell text as printed in Margoliouth's edition of the Oxford English Texts, Volume II (1958). Volume I, Introduction, pp.xii-xvii, should be consulted for further information about the manuscripts. Margoliouth has printed the poems from the two manuscripts side by side. For a clearer setting out of the Dobell sequence the reader is referred to the edition of Gladys Wade (1932, repr. 1962).

1. Quoted from Day, *Thomas Traherne*, p.35. *Christian Ethicks* (1675) was one of Traherne's last works and contains his final thoughts on religious philosophy.
2. See Day, pp.9–14.
3. *Centuries* or *Centuries of Meditations* is probably the most popular of Traherne's works, written during the last five years of his life, as were his other works. Quoted from Margoliouth, I, 226.
4. See Wade, pp.253–4 for the original version and Philip Traherne's revision.
5. The 'Golden Chain' or *Catena Aurea* is part of orthodox Thomist philosophy.
6. This was changed by Philip Traherne in the Dobell Folio but the similes are retained. See Wade, p.251.

Chapter 7

1. For the meaning of 'theme' see Chapter 3. note 5.

2. Phonaesthesia: the study of the expressiveness of sounds. See Katie Wales, *A Dictionary of Stylistics* (London: Longman, 1989), pp.352–3. For a recent study of phonaesthetics see Walter Nash, 'Sound and the pattern of poetic meaning' in D'haen, T., ed., *Linguistics and the Study of Literature* (Amsterdam: Rodopi, 1986).

3. For this category of verb see Quirk et al., *A Comprehensive Grammar of the English Language* (London: Longman, 1985), paras. 4.28 & 4.32.

Chapter 8

1. See Gardner, *Divine Poems*, 2nd ed., pp.138–47. In an essay on the problems of dating the verses, she suggests that they were in fact written and sent to Herbert earlier than the seal, possibly c.1615, when he was seeking secular preferment.

2. See Partridge, *John Donne: Language and Style*, p.92.

3. See Legouis, *Donne the Craftsman*, p.23.

Select Bibliography and Further Reading

Texts

Crashaw, Richard, *The Poems English Latin and Greek of Richard Crashaw*, ed. L. C. Martin (Oxford: Clarendon Press, 1927, 2nd ed. 1957, repr. 1966).

Donne, John, *The Divine Poems*, ed. Helen Gardner (Oxford: Clarendon Press, 1952, 2nd ed. 1978).

Donne, John, *The Elegies and The Songs and Sonnets*, ed. Helen Gardner (Oxford: Clarendon Press, 1965, repr. 1978).

Donne, John, *The Epithalamions, Anniversaries and Epicedes*, ed. W. Milgate (Oxford: Clarendon Press, 1978).

Donne, John, *The Satires, Epigrams and Verse Letters*, ed. W. Milgate (Oxford: Clarendon Press, 1967).

Donne, John, *The Songs and Sonets of John Donne*, ed. Theodore Redpath (London: Methuen, 1956, repr. University Paperback Series, 1967).

Herbert, George, *The Works of George Herbert*, ed. F. E. Hutchinson (Oxford: Clarendon Press, 1941, repr. rev. 1967).

Traherne, Thomas, *Centuries, Poems, and Thanksgivings*, 2 vols, ed. H. M. Margoliouth (Oxford: Clarendon Press, 1958). Volume I *Introduction and Centuries*, Volume II *Poems and Thanksgivings*.

Traherne, Thomas, *The Poetical Works of Thomas Traherne*, ed. Gladys I. Wade (London: P. J. & A. E. Dobell, 3rd ed. 1932, repr. 1962) [N.B. 1st and 2nd eds (1903 & 1906) – with modernized spelling – ed. Bertram Dobell].

Vaughan, Henry, *The Works of Henry Vaughan*, ed. L. C. Martin (Oxford: Clarendon Press, 1914, 2nd ed. 1957).

Vaughan, Henry, *Henry Vaughan: The Complete Poems*, ed. Alan Rudrum (Newhaven & London. Yale University Press, 1981, 1st pub. by Penguin Books Ltd, 1976).

General Studies

Bennett, Joan, *Five Metaphysical Poets* (Cambridge: Cambridge University Press, 1964).
——, *Four Metaphysical Poets* (Cambridge: Cambridge University Press, 2nd ed. 1953, 1st pub. 1934).
Freeman, Rosemary, *English Emblem Books* (New York: Octagon Books, 1966, 1st pub. 1948).
Hammond, Gerald, (ed.), *The Metaphysical Poets* (London: Macmillan, 1974, repr. 1986).
Martines, Lauro, *Society and History in English Renaissance Verse* (Oxford: Basil Blackwell, 1985).
Miner, Earl, *The Metaphysical Mode from Donne to Cowley* (Princeton, New Jersey: Princeton University Press, 1969).
Parfitt, George, *English Poetry of the Seventeenth Century* (London: Longman, 1985).
Peterson, Douglas L., *The English Lyric from Wyatt to Donne* (Princeton, New Jersey: Princeton University Press, 1967).
Praz, Mario, *Studies in Seventeenth-Century Imagery* (Rome: Edizione di Storia e Letteretura, 1939, 2nd ed. 1964).
Quarles, Francis, *Emblemes* (London: 1635).
Seelig, Sharon Cadman, *The Shadow of Eternity: Belief and Structure in Herbert, Vaughan and Traherne* (Lexington, Kentucky: University of Kentucky Press, 1981).
Sloane, Mary Cole, *The Visual in Metaphysical Poetry* (New Jersey: Humanities Press Inc., 1981).
Tillyard, E. M. W., *The Elizabethan World Picture* (London: Chatto and Windus, 1943. Pub. in Penguin Books 1963).
Tuve, Rosamond, *Elizabethan and Metaphysical Imagery* (Chicago: University of Chicago Press, 1947).
Willey, Basil, *The Seventeenth Century Background* (London: Chatto and Windus, 1934. Pub. in Penguin Books 1962).

Donne

Legouis, Pierre, *Donne the Craftsman* (New York: Russell & Russell, 1962, 1st pub. 1928).
Leishman, J. B., *Monarch of Wit* (London: Hutchinson, 1951, 6th ed. 1962).
Partridge, A. C., *John Donne: Language and Style* (London: André Deutsch, 1978).
Roberts, John R. (ed.), *Essential Articles for the Study of John Donne's Poetry* (Hamden, Connecticut: Archon Books, 1975).
Rugoff, Milton Allan, *Donne's Imagery: A Study in Creative Sources* (New York: Russell & Russell, 1962, 1st pub. 1939).
Smith, A. J. (ed.), *John Donne the Critical Heritage* (London: Routledge & Kegan Paul, 1975).

Warnke, Frank J., *John Donne* (Boston, Mass.: Twayne Publishers, 1987).
Winny, James, *A Preface to Donne* (London: Longman, 1970).

Herbert

Edgecombe, Rodney, *'Sweetnesse Readie Penn'd': Imagery, Syntax and Metrics in the Poetry of George Herbert* (Salzburg: University of Salzburg, 1980).
Patrides, C.A. (ed.), *George Herbert the Critical Heritage* (London: Routledge & Kegan Paul, 1983).
Roberts, John R. (ed.), *Essential Articles for the Study of George Herbert's Poetry* (Hamden, Connecticut: Archon Books, 1979).
Tuve, Rosamund, *A Reading of George Herbert* (London: Faber & Faber, 1952).

Crashaw

Bertonasco, Marc F., *Crashaw and the Baroque* (Alabama: University of Alabama Press, 1971).
Cooper, Robert M. (ed.), *Essays on Richard Crashaw* (Salzburg: University of Salzburg, 1979).
Parrish, Paul A., *Richard Crashaw* (Boston, Mass.: Twayne Publishers, 1980).
Wallerstein, Ruth C., *Richard Crashaw: A Study in Style and Poetic Development* (Madison: University of Wisconsin Press, 1959, 1st pub. 1935).
Warren, Austin, *Richard Crashaw: A Study in Baroque Sensibility* (London: Faber & Faber, 1939).

Vaughan

Calhoun, Thomas O., *Henry Vaughan: The Achievement of Silex Scintillans* (London: Associated University Presses, 1981).
Friedenreich, Kenneth, *Henry Vaughan* (Boston, Mass.: Twayne Publishers, 1978).
Holmes, Elizabeth, *Henry Vaughan and the Hermetic Philosophy* (Oxford: Basil Blackwell, 1932).
Hutchinson, F. E., *Henry Vaughan A Life and Interpretation* (Oxford: Clarendon Press, 1947).
Rudrum, Alan (ed.), *Essential Articles for the Study of Henry Vaughan* (Hamden, Connecticut: Archon Books, 1987).

Traherne

Day, Malcolm, *Thomas Traherne* (Boston, Mass.: Twayne Publishers, 1982).

Salter, K.W., *Thomas Traherne: Mystic and Poet* (London: Edward Arnold, 1964).

Wade, Gladys I., *Thomas Traherne* (Princeton, New Jersey: Princeton University Press, 1944).

Index 1 Literary and Historical References

Note Numbers at the end of a series, written thus: 2.4, refer to the Notes. 2.4 would indicate: Notes, Chapter 2, note 4.

Adam of St Victor, 3.3
Alciati, Andrea, 1.8
Anglican (Church), 3–5, 48–9
Aquinas, Thomas (Thomist), 176, 6.5
Armada (Spanish), 1

Bacon, Francis, 1, 14
Barnes, William, 24
Bedford, Lucy, Countess of, 155–7
Bemerton, 4, 49
Bible, 2, 47–8, 53, 100, 112–14, 130–1, 138–9, 162, 5.8
Biblia Pauperum, 47, 3.12
Blake, William, 145
Book of Common Prayer (Liturgy), 47, 49, 61, 75, 138, 5.8, 5.9
Books of Hours, 47, 3.12, 5.7
Bridgeman, Sir Orlando, 3–4, 176–7
Bunyan, John, 3, 67

Cambridge Platonists, 127, 153, 176–7
Catholic, Roman, 1–4, 46, 170
Cavalier poets, 2
Charles I, 2–3
Charles II, 2–3
Civil War, 1–2, 4, 176

Columbus, Christopher, 2.6
Commonwealth, 1–3, 14
Copernicus, Nicolaus, 1–2, 19
Coverdale, Miles, 5.8

Denham, Sir John, 5.9
Descartes, René, 2, 176
Dryden, John, 3

Egerton, Sir Thomas, 4
Elizabeth I, 2
Elizabethan, thought etc., 6, 7–8, 10–11, 14–16, 21, 42, 46, 151, 168, 172–3, 179
Emblem Books, 11–12, 14, 67

Galen, 173
Galileo Galilei, 1, 19, 2.1
Glanvill, Joseph, 176
Glorious Revolution, 1
Greene, Robert, 20

Harvey, Gabriel, 20
Harvey, William, 20, 2.2
Henrietta Maria, Queen, 4
Herbals, 50, 3.2
Herbert, Magdalen, 166
Hermetic philosophy (hermeticism), 111, 113, 127, 153, 162, 172–6, 5.1

190 INDEX

Heywood, Thomas, 107
Hobbes, Thomas, 1–2, 176
Hopkins, Gerard Manley, 24, 105

Inns of Court, 6, 1.4

James I, 4
James II, 5

Loreto, Italy, 4
Lumen de Lumine, 5.2

Marino, Giambattista, 75, 4.1
Martial, 10
Mary II, 5
Milton, John, 2–3, 19, 77, 89, 112, 4.6

Nashe, Thomas, 20
Nollius, Henricius, 173

Ovid, 40

Paracelsus, Theophrastus, 173
Pembroke, Mary, Countess of, *see* Sidney, Mary
Petrarch, Francesco, 6–7, 21, 40
Plantin, Christopher, 12
Platonism, Cambridge, *see* Cambridge Platonists
Pope, Alexander, 112
Ptolemaic universe, 19
Puritan, 2, 4, 5

Quarles, Francis, 14, 41, 67, 71, 95, 1.10, 2.8, 4.7

Randolph, Thomas, 5.9
Ralegh, Sir Walter, 6
Restoration, 2, 3, 166
Royalist, 4, 5
Royal Society, 1, 176

Shakespeare, William, 6, 8–9, 14–15, 81, 160, 167, 5.2
Sidney, Mary, Countess of Pembroke, 8, 1.5
Sidney, Sir Philip, 6–11, 13, 15–17, 57
Speculum humanae salvationis, 47, 3.12
Spenser, Edmund, 2, 6, 8, 12, 57, 112, 1.6

Traherne, Philip, 137–8, 148, 150, 166, 183, 6.6

Vaughan, Thomas, 5.2

Wales (Welsh), 3–4, 104–5, 107, 5.4, 5.5
Walton, Izaak, 1, 49, 110, 166
Whichcote, Benjamin, 176
Whitney, Geoffrey, 12
William II, 5
Wilson, Thomas, 15
Wyatt, Sir Thomas, 6, 16

Index 2 Language Topics

adjectives, 24, 52, 60, 76, 78, 80–2, 93, 95, 109, 111, 116, 116–7, 130, 131, 134, 136, 162–3, 168, 170, 2.5
   abstract, 24, 130, 131, 140, 168
   adjective phrase, 87
   as pro-forms, 158
   compound adjectives, 24–5, 52, 79, 156
adverbs and adverbial adjuncts, xi–xii, 25, 57, 64, 77, 86–7, 87, 117, 134, 158
   adverbial clauses, *see* clauses, adverbial
allegory, 67, 102–3, 161
ambiguity, 36–7, 73, 118, 168
anaphoric reference, 26, 119, 124, 143–4, 157, 158
apposition, 57, 85, 92–3, 107, 145, 3.6
articles and determiners, 31, 62, 110–11, 170–1

cataphoric reference, 26, 27, 31, 44
circumlocution, 80, 93
classical allusions, 7, 83, 97, 139
clauses, 34–8, 54–7, 85–7, 119–21, 142–5
   adverbial, 61–2
   adversative, 55
   asyndetic, 64, 85, 89, 159
   comment, 125
   co-ordinate, 55, 55–6, 89, 118, 119–20, 142–4, 159
   correlative, 86, 117

clauses—*continued*
   interpolated, *see* interpolation
   length of, 34–5, 38, 54, 59, 62, 85–6, 87, 118, 122, 142–3, 159, 161, 168
   minor and verbless, 60, 86, 92
   non-finite
      past participle, 120, 122–3, 143–4; present participle, 86, 120, 122–3; *to* infinitive, 86, 92, 148
   order of clause elements (S V C), xi, 34, 57, 87, 121, 133, 159, 168
   relative, xi, 55–6, 89, 120, 144, 159
   reported, 16, 38
   subordinate, 56, 86, 88, 89, 118, 142–4, 159
   that clauses, nominal subject, 90
   see also reported clauses
cohesion, *see* texture
complement, xi, 30, 34, 36, 62, 86, 87, 90, 93, 159
conceits, 11, 12, 15, 34, 38–42, 53, 65, 84–5, 88, 107, 168, 2.8, 3.12
conjunctions, 11, 25, 26, 55–6, 57, 63, 64, 85, 89, 119, 120, 122, 156
connectives, 62, 63, 88, 118–19
co-ordination, 59, 111, 117, 131, 144, 159
   see also clauses, co-ordinate
cynghanedd, 105

INDEX

direct address, 16–17, 36, 58, 122–6, 156
dramatic presentation, 16–17, 69–71, 122–6, 170
interior monologue, 17, 70
dyfalu, 104, 107

ellipsis and compression, 26–7, 36–8, 45, 54, 55, 57, 60–1, 73, 86–7, 88, 89, 91–3, 107, 117, 120, 125–6, 146, 156–8, 168, 170, 171
emblems and emblematic language, 11–15, 40–2, 52–3, 66, 67, 69, 71, 73, 76, 78, 84–5, 87, 93–5, 101, 102, 138, 161, 168, 169, 170, 1.8, 1.9, 1.10, 2.8, 3.3, 3.13, 4.7
epigrams, 10, 11, 12, 43, 45, 75, 1.7

functional shift, 33, 101, 116, 117–18

imagery and figurative language, 46, 47, 49, 66, 67, 72–3, 74, 87, 94, 98, 108–9, 148, 150–1, 169–71
see also conceits, emblems, rhetoric
images, sources of, *see also* language, types of
botany, 18
business and commerce, 18, 50, 83–4
colour, 109–10, 131
cosmology and astronomy, 19, 156, 160
garden, 50, 73
geography, 18, 40, 2.7
household, 23–4, 49, 72–4, 104
law, 19, 21–2
man-made objects, 134, 135, 136
medicine and anatomy, 18, 19–20, 104, 110, 133, 135

images, sources of—*continued*
music, 49, 65–6
nature, 23, 104, 110–13, 161–2, 170
philosophy, 19, 83, 111, 113–14, 116, 152–3, 162, 6.5
physical world, 108–9, 115, 130, 133, 136–7
precious stones, 130, 135–6, 137
science and pseudo-science, 18, 51, 162
sea, 51
sport, 51
topical interest, 18, 40, 51, 126, 156
trades and occupations, 51, 52, 104
war, 18–19, 51, 84–5, 126
intensifiers, 131, 132, 144
interpolation
clauses, 34, 35, 56, 87, 120, 123
phrases, 36, 87
inversion, 28, 29, 34, 43, 56–7, 88, 121, 133, 146, 158, 159—60, 168
see also thematic marking
language, types of
archaic and obsolescent, 7, 112
argument and reasoning, 9, 10, 11, 15, 25, 26–8, 39, 46, 169, 171
associative, 76, 77–8, 80–2, 101–2, 109, 135–7, 140, 162
baroque, 76, 79, 99, 170
biblical, 47–8, 97–8, 101, 107, 112–13, 114–15, 126, 131, 138–9, 151, 162
colloquial, 7, 8, 20, 59–60, 83, 106–7, 125
conversational, 7, 123–6, 161
courtly and eloquent, 7, 9, 17, 53
dramatic, 16, 17, 123–6, 167
elevated and literary, 83, 95, 112, 170, 5.9
epigrammatic, 10, 11, 12, 15, 26–7, 43, 45, 75, 86

language, types of—*continued*
  liturgical, 47, 48–9, 53, 138, 3.7
  logic and syllogistic, 10, 11, 15, 39, 169
  lyric, 20–1, 23, 47, 77, 107, 145, 146, 150
  'negative', 130, 134, 136
  pastoral, 8, 9, 17, 112
  'plain', 6, 7, 8, 9, 53, 168, 169
  proverbial, 7, 126
  riddling, 9–10, 42, 43, 45, 46, 52–3, 67, 92–3, 98, 150
    see also word play
  sensuous and erotic, 77, 94, 98–9, 150–1
  speech-based, 16, 17, 125, 167
    see also speech, representation of
  statement, 27–8
  stylized, 112–13, 126, 136

metre, 16, 18, 25, 28, 30–1, 34–8, 59, 85, 110, 117, 122, 125, 145, 161, 167
  caesura, 26, 29, 35, 110, 117, 122, 125, 143, 157

nominal groups, xi, 24, 26, 35, 57, 62, 85, 93, 107, 145
  nonmodification, 110–11, 136–7
  premodification, xi, 62, 79, 80–1, 93, 111, 116, 117, 131, 136
  postmodification, xi, 62, 69, 86, 87, 89, 93, 117, 118, 120, 122–3
nouns, xi, 52, 76, 77, 141–2, 162, 168, 2.5
  abstract, 22, 116, 139–40, 141–2
  concrete, 23, 130, 133, 135

parallelism, 37, 37–8, 118–19, 121, 143, 147–8
parenthesis, 56, 87, 125–6
Petrarchan allusions, 21, 40

prepositions, 25, 32, 88
prepositional complements, 93
prepositional phrases
  adverbial, 93, 119–20
  postmodifying, xi, 62, 93, 117
pro-forms, 26–7, 28, 31–2, 34, 36–7, 60, 92–3, 157–9
pronouns, 25, 26, 30–3, 92–3, 142
  compound, 33
  definite, 31–2, 158 (*such*)
  demonstrative, 26, 27, 31, 119
    as pro-forms, 26, 31, 119, 158
  indefinite, 26, 32, 43
  independent possessive, 36–7, 142, 157
  interrogative, 33, 156
  personal, 7, 26, 30–1, 60, 103, 124, 156, 157–8
    as pro-forms, 26
  possessive, 31, 62
  relative, 33

repetition, 15, 16–17, 42–6, 67–9, 132, 142, 146, 170, 3.14
  clauses, 68, 89
  parts of speech, 44–5, 122, 142
  phrases, 147
  sounds, 68, 69, 88, 95–6, 105–6, 164
  syntactic frames, 89–91, 132, 147–8
  words, 43, 44, 64, 67, 68, 91, 132, 142, 147, 150
rhetoric, 15, 18, 46, 67, 88, 159–60
rhetorical figures
  alliteration, 7, 55, 69, 70, 81, 95–6, 105–6, 107, 117, 150
  anadiplosis, 68, 69, 91
  anaphora, 91
  antimetabole, 16, 43, 45
  apostrophe, 11, 80, 85, 124, 142
  chiasmus, 16, 43, 68, 77, 89, 157–9
  epizeuxis, 68
  exclamation, 85, 86, 144–5

rhetorical figures—*continued*
  hyperbole, 39, 132
  metaphor, 11, 15, 18, 24, 38–9,
    42, 49, 62, 64–7, 71–3,
    77, 78, 83, 85, 88, 93–4,
    97, 103–4, 132, 135, 140,
    145, 148–9, 160–1, 168,
    169, 170
  metonymy, 73
  onomatopoeia, 88, 163
  oxymoron, 79
  paradox, 10, 11, 42, 43, 45, 46,
    79, 86, 98, 99, 105,
    143–4, 150, 152, 157,
    168, 170, 171, 2.11
  personification, 12, 69–71, 97
  ploce, 67
  polyptoton, 43, 45, 46, 53, 67–8,
    157
  pun, 15, 42, 53, 69, 71, 135
  repetition *see* repetition
  simile, 11, 18, 21, 25, 39, 42,
    73–4, 97, 104, 118–19,
    120–1, 132, 149–50,
    156–9
rhyme, 29, 35, 36, 54, 59, 61–2,
    63–4, 76, 105, 122, 145–7,
    164, 167–8, 5.5
rhythm, 17, 21, 35, 58–9, 73–4,
    85, 86, 88, 110–11, 121–2,
    123, 125, 145–7, 167–8

sentence structure, 34–8, 55–6,
  85–7, 87–93, 119–23, 142–8,
  159–60
  clause complexes, xii, 35, 55,
    86, 120, 123, 144, 168
  resumption, 37–8, 68, 89–91,
    159
sentence types
  exclamations, 58, 85, 118, 132,
    142, 144–5, 161
  imperatives, 54, 61, 65, 118,
    122–3
  questions, 28, 58, 85, 89, 118,
    132, 142
  statements, 27–8, 85, 105–6,
    118, 132, 142–3

sound, 95–7, 105–7, 122, 163, 164,
  5.5, 7.2
  assonance, 105–6, 164, 5.5
  'consonantal chime', 105–6, 164
  repetition of, *see* repetition,
    sounds
speech, representation of, 16–17,
  35, 36, 57–60, 70–1, 125
speech fillers, 58, 60, 125
stanza forms, 35, 54, 55, 58–9,
  63–4, 85, 87, 121–2, 145–7,
  167–8
stress, 16, 17, 25, 26, 27, 28, 29,
  30, 31, 32, 33, 34, 35, 38, 44,
  45, 59, 117, 147, 156, 157,
  158, 162
substitution, 62
  see also pro-forms
syllogism, *see* language, types of:
  logic
symbolism, 47–8, 49, 53, 67, 74,
  76, 95, 101, 168, 170
  see also emblems

texture and cohesion, 62–7, 88–9,
  160, 161, 167, 3.9
thematic marking, 56, 68, 159
  explanation of, 3.5

verbs and verbal groups, *see also*
  clauses, xi, 22, 25–30, 27, 52,
    55, 61–2, 77–8, 87, 116, 122,
    131–2, 140–2, 163, 168, 2.5,
    7.3
  auxiliary, xi, 26–9, 38, 44, 87
    as pro-forms, 26–7, 28, 158–9
    modal auxiliaries, 26–7, 45
    primary auxiliaries, 28
  be, lexically full, xi, 28–9, 141,
    157, 158
  copular and lexically empty, xi,
    28–9, 34, 77
  do, lexically full, 28–9, 33, 141
  dynamic, 29, 44–5, 77, 95, 116,
    132, 140, 141, 163
  ellipted, 60, 146, 159
  finite, 92, 131–2

verbs and verbal groups—*continued*
  infinitive as pro-form, 27
  participles used adjectivally, 111, 116
  phrasal, 59–60, 107
  relational, 29, 30
  stance, 163
  stative, 29, 30, 78, 132, 140–1, 163
    attitudinal, 78
    cognitive, 29, 132, 141
    inert perception, 29, 132, 140–1, 163
  transitive, 107, 116
vocabulary, *see also* language
  abstract, 9, 22, 24, 34, 38, 52, 130–1, 139–40, 142, 170, 171
  archaic, 7, 112
  colloquial, 7, 8, 20, 59–60, 83, 106–7, 125
  compounds, 24–5, 52, 79, 116, 150, 156

vocabulary—*continued*
  concrete, 23, 24, 38, 46, 52, 76, 94–5, 130–1, 133, 169, 171
  'flat', 7, 9
  grammatical or lexically empty, 25, 25–34, 37, 38, 42, 43, 46, 142, 157, 159
  Latin and Romance, 7, 21–2, 76, 82–3, 95, 111, 115–16, 142, 150, 156, 157, 168
  learned and literary, 83, 95, 170
  lexically full, 43, 141, 147
  monosyllables, 7, 22–3, 24, 25, 76, 83, 107, 156, 163, 168, 2.4
  native, 24, 76, 82–3, 107, 115–6, 150, 156, 168, 169
  technical, 51, 65, 114

word play, 32, 43, 53, 66, 98, 105, 150
  see also language, types of: riddling